The SureWealth Way

Escape from Wall Street and discover strategies for More Wealth with less Worry!

Andy Daniels

Contents

Preface 1

Introduction – Confessions of a Former "Typical" Financial Planner 5

Chapter 1 – The Truth about Typical Financial Planning and Advice 12

Chapter 2 – Financial Insanity 20

Chapter 3 – How Did We Get Here? 36

Chapter 4 – The SureWealth Way 57

Chapter 5 – The 10 Truths of the SureWealth Way 62

Chapter 6 – SureWealth in Action 75

Chapter 7 – What Now? 114

Meet the Authors 119

Preface

In 2015, I was introduced to the world of non-traditional financial strategies, which would reshape my approach to economic security and growth. Seeking a reliable way to plan for retirement, I ventured beyond the conventional routes and discovered a set of financial concepts that promised more control, flexibility, and growth potential than traditional options. What I discovered laid the groundwork for a sustainable, independent economic future.

At the time, my wife and I had two children under five years old. (Now we have five!) I worked in Human Resources recruiting for a multi-billion dollar scientific research institute; my wife worked in organizational leadership development.

We learned how to turn our vision for the future into a verifiable, step-by-step roadmap to achieve our financial goals. With a combination of a retirement analyzer, financial

software, and policy illustrations, we were given a simple financial roadmap that was easy to understand yet detailed enough to give us confidence.

The roadmap gave us the confidence to push forward with our life goals, knowing we had results we could count on with a bedrock foundation for financial security. The strategies guaranteed we would have more money each year than the last. It also protected us against "worst-case scenarios" so that we could reach our goals under any circumstance. All we had to do was simply follow the steps.

This roadmap allowed us to save reliably while also having flexibility and spending freedom. **Now, my family is living the life we have chosen.** We have the confidence to live our lives (and even spend) knowing that our future is secure.

Best yet, the strategies have delivered results **precisely as planned.** There have been no surprises or disruptions in our progress. No market conditions, not even the pandemic, interrupted our financial gain and peace of mind.

These "SureWealth" strategies, as we now call this approach, allow us to enjoy life without stressing over money. The roadmap has even allowed us to expand our family to five children (our last two were twins), knowing that we could be confident in our financial future.

Even after we implemented our unique set of strategies, I took time to investigate other potential options thoroughly. I couldn't find anything else to match the system we discovered regarding security and confidence. Knowing this, I couldn't help but share it with my friends and family! As I shared what I had learned, others soon began wanting what my family was having. It was then that I started helping them implement SureWealth strategies.

As friends and family began to have success, I was motivated to share with people beyond my immediate circle. It was profound, helping people rediscover the art of saving and combining that with financial strategies that eliminated the roller coaster ride of the stock market.

Today, I am "all in," helping others. It's been my privilege to help further develop the SureWealth philosophy, strategies, and tools to spread the message to a broader audience.

I have learned this along the way: **You don't have to accept what Wall Street is dishing out, with all the uncertainty and stress that comes with it.** The system has failed, and it's time to stop trusting it with your dollars.

If you desire peace of mind, predictability, and stability in your finances, you'll want to read on. And if, like me, you don't want to wait until you're **retired** to enjoy your wealth, I encourage you to read this entire book. It may go against the grain of what you've been told, but chances are, once explained, it will make complete sense. As a matter of fact, once you see it, you can't un-see it.

You may have noticed, like I did, that Wall Street and typical financial strategies offer no Guarantees. (Well, the guarantee is that *they* always come out on top, regardless of how the "main street" investors fare!) You may have watched friends who thought they were set for retirement scramble for work to bolster portfolio losses. You might have suffered sleepless nights and unnecessary stress, wondering what the financial markets would do next. However, you can educate yourself and take your power back.

Most people resign themselves to the risk and volatility of the market in a system designed to make only those at the top very rich. But the SureWealth strategies are designed to help *you* rise above the challenges and escape the system.

You ***can*** create financial stability, security, and prosperity for yourself and your family. You ***can*** build wealth—no matter what happens with the stock market, housing market, interest rates, or economy. This book will show you how.

—Andy Daniels
SureWealth Solutions

INTRODUCTION

Confessions of a Former "Typical" Financial Planner

Two decades ago, I left typical financial planning. I had come into it with high expectations and new suits. I wasn't worried about the risks and fees associated with  typical planning because I didn't know I should be worried. All I knew was that I had passed the testing and was now educated in the ways of Wall Street! I now had the "magic bullet" that would make everyone rich.

To make a long story short, I learned the hard way that putting money in the market and trusting everything would be great was a big mistake. This system required the utmost trust of Wall Street and minimum control of one's destiny. It became clear that the system was broken, and soon, I no longer wanted to be a part of it.

I abandoned the typical financial advice I had been doling out, even calling clients to let them know the advice I had given them was mistaken. Then, I started getting a real education on ways to create reliable, usable wealth through proven, verifiable strategies that successful people have used for years.

Why did I humble myself and make such a drastic change?

Because I no longer felt that "typical" financial planning advice allowed me to do what was best for my clients.

I had come to believe that what we were telling clients was, at best, misleading and, at worst, flat-out wrong.

To give you a peek behind the curtain, let me tell you what it's like in a typical financial planning office.

Clients would come in with questions. "How much do I need to save?" "Where should I invest?" "Will I have enough money to last?"

In turn, we asked them questions. "When do you want to retire?" "What kind of income and lifestyle do you want?" "What's your risk tolerance?" And 20 more questions the clients often needed help to answer accurately from where they sat.

However, we didn't ask them to anticipate colossal stock market crashes, divorce, or disruptions in employment.

First, the client would guess when they might want to retire, how much they could save, and so on. Then, as advisors, we would make guesses and assumptions about how much their investments might earn and what future costs, taxes, and inflation might be. (And nobody ever estimated 9% inflation!)

Next, we'd plug all of our guesses into a computer. Then, using the firm's impressive number-crunching, graph-generating software, we'd create impressive full-color illustrations and deliver their "financial plan" in a beautiful binder.

The people who received them felt reassured that they were "on track." They'd thank us. They'd start writing checks. And the boss would congratulate us.

But it was pure guesswork. (Theirs and mine.)

It was an insane system, all based on erroneous assumptions. The questions and answers helped us build a relationship and create trust with the client, but did we deserve their trust? It's absurd to imagine we could accurately predict their income, the impact of future taxation, account for inflation, and plan for children's college costs, all while anticipating the market.

When do mere assumptions remain constant for 25, 30, or 40+ years? Who hasn't had their "best-laid plans" disrupted by unforeseen realities?

Often a bit nervous about the future, most clients were relieved to get advice. They followed recommendations willingly, even if those recommendations mainly consisted of putting money in the stock market every month and hoping it all worked out.

I knew I couldn't guarantee their financial success any more than I could guarantee the weather. I knew we were giving people false hopes and telling them things we had no business telling them.

I just couldn't do it anymore.

This book tells why I turned my business model upside down, abandoned my series 6 and 63 licenses I had worked so hard to earn, and struck out on my own. It's why I no longer manage assets or sell mutual funds and how I help clients discover a better way to prepare for their future.

This book is also an introduction to a genuine alternative to Financial Planning. The SureWealth Way is a set of principles, philosophies, and strategies that work. Many wealthy people I have known and observed have used these strategies, but it's not the plan Wall Street promotes.

Your bankers and financial planners will never tell you the information I'm about to share.

To begin with, they probably don't even know it or understand it. (And let's be honest, most people doing "financial planning" are salespeople.)

Financial planners may be well-educated and have letters after their names. (I know I was, and I did.) They may even charge a fee for their advice. But they're operating from a skewed, limited perspective, and I had to come to terms with that.

I realized that perhaps I was just well-taught to believe in (and not to question) the products and strategies I was selling. But, like many other well-meaning advisors, it didn't occur to me that there were other options. *Better options.*

I had to go searching. When I did, I discovered those better options. They were the principles and strategies that have helped people build *sustainable* wealth for many decades, even centuries before "financial planning" even existed.

I'll share more about that alternative and why I found it necessary in the first place, but first, I am grateful that you've found your way to this book. This book and the following resources will allow you to see things differently.

Before I go on to the next chapter, I have a few simple requests to make.

First, I encourage you to read this entire book. Read it right now or within the next 24 hours. Whether the perspective is new to you or just a reminder of what you already know, I encourage you not to let the low *price* of this information dilute its *value*.

Second, keep an open mind if (or when) the information I present contradicts what you already believe or know. Then, try on the ideas, do your research, and consider if there might not be alternatives worth trying other than "typical" financial strategies and advice.

Third, don't sabotage yourself with resistance. I know that financial books can come across as "sales-y" when the authors have services or products to offer. But don't let that stop you from educating yourself! My team and I have strived to ensure this book is helpful to anyone—whether or not we ever work together. Bottom line: we want to empower as many people as possible!

Lastly, please don't "just" read this book. Take action! Your money and your future depend on it. Whether you decide to work with me or someone else, I ask that you do something to move toward a prosperous, peace-filled life. It's a journey worth taking.

If you read this book and decide that the SureWealth Way makes more sense than typical financial planning, contact us (or the person who gave you this book) to start aligning your finances for increased wealth and security.

If you're tired of crossing your fingers and hoping that the stock market doesn't crash, but don't know what else to do; we have answers for you.

We're part of a grassroots movement of agents, advisors, investors, and consumers taking back our thinking and our money from the institutions and corporations that too often put their profits first and their client's best interests in the backseat.

We represent a different way to create and keep wealth. It is a less-traveled, proven path to help you build wealth with greater confidence, more certainty, and less worry. We advocate this alternative path because the truth is this:

Typical financial advice—compliments of Wall Street—has failed.

It's time to get honest about what's gone wrong and discover a better way.

CHAPTER 1

The Truth about Typical Financial Planning and Advice

I entered the financial planning field with gusto, optimism, and the enthusiasm of a true believer. At first, a career in financial planning was  what I had hoped for exactly—a chance to be successful by helping people financially. But over time, disillusionment set in.

Financial planning sounded like a good idea, and it's certainly better than nothing. But as I learned, it was based on best guesses, dated assumptions, unfounded optimism, and mathematical half-truths.

People believe they can expect to earn certain returns in the stock market. Some financial gurus even assure people they'll make an average return of 12% over time in the stock market, which is not based on reality, especially after fees, commissions, and other costs.

Clients are told about the wonders of compounding interest but rarely about:

- How costs also compound over time.
- How fees create lost opportunity costs that grow larger than the fees themselves.
- How "average" rates of return don't equal "actual" rates of return.
- When "target-date" funds regularly fail to protect investors from risk as promised.
- Why speed trading and other Wall St. shenanigans make today's market significantly more volatile than the stock market in which our parents invested.

Furthermore, investors are encouraged to defer taxes without seriously considering their potential impact when they need the money later. Investors are also assured "your tax rate will be lower when you retire," when the opposite might be true. (Who thinks taxes are going down or that they'll be easier to pay after you stop working? And who wants less income anyway: why not more?)

Then there is the math. It's a cruel lie for most people to believe they can work for 40 years, save a small percentage of their income, then quit work and "retire" for decades of high inflation. Yet this is the cultural expectation, what we think is "supposed" to happen.

So many investors believe this is what they must do: contribute to their 401(k)s, cross their fingers, and just "hope" that the market does its magic and not its damage.

Unfortunately, there are no guarantees. Financial planners can only hope that things will work out and that the market returns might enable clients to reach financial independence. (But who wants that kind of risk?)

We offer an alternative approach: the SureWealth Way.

We meet with clients to show them how to make an actual plan with current expenses, inflation, returns, guarantees, future inflows, and outflows that represent your real numbers, now and in the future.

Many planners will show you hypothetical illustrations and examples that may look different from your situation. However, you have the right to understand the actual numbers - your numbers. We call it "financial forecasting," and it is the opposite of throwing money at Wall Street and "hoping." (More on this later…)

It's time to tell the TRUTH about financial planning, retirement, and the markets we believe will save us.

The TRUTH is that typical financial planning is based on speculation and wishful thinking.

The TRUTH is that even when people believe they are "on track," they are generally under-saving.

The TRUTH is that, right now, millionaires who have followed typical financial advice are afraid to spend their principal for fear of outliving their savings.

The TRUTH is that many people will eventually become dependent on the government or family.

The TRUTH is that most "typical" planners and brokers cross their fingers and pray that the stock market doesn't crash *because they don't know what else to do.*

And the problems go DEEPER than unrealistic expectations and optimistic math.

The TRUTH is that the current system rewards financial planners and advisors for convincing clients to put and keep their money at risk!

It's just how the system works. Advisors and money managers get paid for "assets under management." And those assets are typically at risk in the market. Then there are all the "half-truths." (And un-truths)

Conventional wisdom says, "Get a good job and max out your 401(k)," but building true wealth this way is rare.

The focus is all on accumulation, even though people must live on cash flow.

Hard-working savers are persuaded to buy cars with cash and pay off their mortgages early instead of putting extra dollars to work building cash-flowing assets.

Financial gurus preach, "Buy term insurance and invest the difference." However, many wealthy and successful people throughout history have done—and still do—the opposite. (Sometimes, the best answer to the whole life vs. term debate is "both.")

Retirement is assumed instead of the possibility that people might be passionately productive at any age.

Diligent retirement savers are programmed to believe they'll somehow spend less in retirement despite inflation and lifestyle desires. (As a buddy of mine is fond of saying, "Every day is Saturday, and you're supposed to spend less?")

Financial projections assume that retirees will be in a "lower tax bracket" against logic that suggests otherwise.

Then there's "Plan B," when unexpected life events derail even the best of plans.

People need money when the job market, the stock market, the marriages, or the rental houses don't go as planned. And when people need money, they raid their 401(k) or IRAs, incurring penalties, income taxes at an inopportune time, and even backend sales fees.

Retirement accounts make lousy, inefficient emergency funds.

Ironically, the best-laid financial plans sometimes make people LESS prepared to weather an economic storm. In 2019, CNBC reported that 52 percent of Americans had raided their retirement accounts early.[1] And that was before the pandemic! In 2020 alone, nearly 1 out of 3 Americans withdrew or borrowed money from their 401(k) or IRA.[2]

---

[1] https://www.cnbc.com/2019/09/05/half-of-americans-have-raided-their-retirement-savings-early.html
[2] https://401kspecialistmag.com/poll-finds-60-raided-retirement-accounts-during-pandemic/

"Planning" can be a joke because when does everything go as planned? There's a saying, "Man makes his plans, and God laughs." So true!

A few years into my career as an advisor, I came to a hard realization:

Conventional financial advice doesn't work well.

It was hit or miss, depending on market forces, luck, and timing. While it may be better than nothing, the fact is that it's a broken system.

And to keep following the same advice, doing the same things, and expecting a different result is the definition of insanity.

Fortunately, you don't have to participate in Wall Street's broken system.

The TRUTH is that the stock market is NOT the only way to invest.

Your dollars DON'T have to ride a roller coaster ride of volatility.

You can create more CERTAINTY than you imagine.

You don't have to put up with the risk, insecurity, and conflicts of interest that your Wall Street advisors have normalized.

We invite you to explore the SureWealth Way with us.

Read on to discover more about guaranteed strategies for your money. But first, let's uncover precisely how big banks and Wall Street's current "solutions" sabotage your wealth.

Have burning questions? Please email us at info@surewealthllc.com or schedule a consultation here: https://about.thesurewealthway.com/schedule

CHAPTER 2

Financial Insanity

What's so wrong with typical financial advice anyway? Let's explore common problems with typical financial planning and how the SureWealth Way offers an alternative path.

More Risk, Less Control

Typical financial planning assumes that you will lose money. The more you're willing to lose, the faster your portfolio will grow. But is this true?

Risk assessment profiles have conditioned us to think that "safe" or "predictable" equals a low return on investment and high risk equals a high reward. But the more we're willing to tolerate losing, the greater our chance of loss.

Societal conditioning leads us to believe we must take additional risks if we want a chance to earn higher returns, but is this true? Or are there alternatives to stock market risks or cash equivalents that grow at a snail's pace?

Typical financial advice presents limited options. For example, the questions on risk tolerance forms determine the appropriate ratio of "stocks vs. bonds," as if those are the only valuable investments.

But typical advice is predictable: unless you're close to retirement or extremely risk averse, they direct you to invest in stocks or mutual funds.

My risk tolerance is zero. I have no tolerance for losing money - mine or my clients.

Typical financial advice offers you just one option for growing your money - rolling the dice in the Wall Street Casino!

When it comes to your financial future, are you sure you want to rely on speculation, hoping that shareholder prices rise instead of fall?

Or would you prefer investments with predictable gains secured by tangible assets?

SureWealth Solutions offers alternatives such as private lending secured by real estate and annuities provided by top-rated life insurance companies. Such strategies can provide a genuine alternative to—or diversification from—the stock market. Ulcers are not required!

SureWealth strategies don't leave results to chance but utilize proven financial vehicles with reliable results. Returns are predictable, at least within a range. Investments with a track record of substantial losses are not recommended.

"But everyone's doing it!"

Your inner skeptic may ask, "If these lesser-known investments worked, wouldn't everybody be using them?" You may feel you're doing something "risky" or even foolish if you insist on controlling your own money. But remember who creates and manages the narratives about investments?

Begin to notice the significant media advertisers. The corporations that profit from selling risky investments sponsor the financial media that educates and influences investors.

These same Wall Street corporations sponsor government decision-makers as well. For example, during the 2020 elections, Wall Street spent nearly $3 billion on political campaigns and lobbying[3] - that's about 4 million dollars a day.

---

[3] https://www.cnbc.com/2021/04/15/wall-street-spent-2point9-billion-to-influence-washington-during-2020-election.html

Has this improved anything for Americans, or does it only benefit Wall Street? (Of course, you know the answer.) In 2008, people lost a *lot* of money due to "credit default swaps"—an asset few had ever heard of before. Yet we are fed narratives that normalize stock market risk and corporate gambles that crash the economy.

Here are a few things to keep in mind:

You CAN escape the world of speculation, fractional banking, and investments with no real-world backing.

You CAN receive healthy returns and even steady payments with lesser-known Sure Wealth strategies.

Historical safety and performance are often better for these strategies than the (misnamed) "securities" that financial corporations are sell you - with far greater certainty.

SureWealth strategies rely on what works and what's proven—not on the most popular strategies or the easiest products to sell. Sometimes, we work harder to sell the best products because the financial media works overtime to convince you it's normal and necessary to keep your money at risk.

Remember your mother's wisdom when you are choosing between stocks whose price action is out of your control or complex funds requiring a PhD to understand:

"If everyone else jumped off a cliff, does that mean you should, too?"

Your mother was right! Do your research and make your own choices. That's why we encourage you to get the details about SureWealth Solutions.

Book an appointment:
https://go.surewealthway.com/schedule

Ask questions. Invite your current advisors, lawyer, CFP, or accountant. Every strategy we recommend is transparent.

The Qualified Plan Quandary

If you follow the guidance to "max out your 401(k)" (or another government-approved qualified plan), then you would surrender control of your assets to the government, the stock market, and your employer's rules.

You defer income taxes until retirement (when you can afford it least). You give up what could have been lesser capital gains taxes. You pay layered, overblown management fees, which will drain enormous amounts of money from your retirement plan.

Just how much will you pay in fees and taxes? As it is verifiably illustrated with Truth

Concepts calculators, you could pay more in income taxes and fees than your total contributions to your retirement plan!

Deferring taxes in a qualified plan means paying taxes on the harvest rather than "the seed."

If you were a farmer...

Would you rather pay taxes on your "penny" seeds or your "million dollar" harvest?

1¢ $1 million

Pay taxes on the seed?
- Reduced total tax burden
- No taxes at retirement
- Today's tax rate

Pay taxes on the harvest?
- Increased tax burden
- Taxes delayed until retirement
- Future unknown (higher?) tax rate
- Required minimum distributions

In the calculator image on the next page, you'll see what happens to $100k over 30 years in a qualified plan. Assuming a tax rate of 20% (now and later), you'll defer 20% or $20,000 in taxes to a future date. That's nice in the short run. But what happens later?

As the account grows—we assumed gains of 8% per year and fees of 1.5%—at the end of 30 years, you would owe ten times the taxes! And that's if tax rates don't increase, which you have no control over.

Down the road, when you are retired and may not have active income, you'll pay $215,759 in taxes, plus more than $147k in management fees. (And the longer you take to draw down your account, the higher your taxes and fees will be.) Does that seem like a good deal?

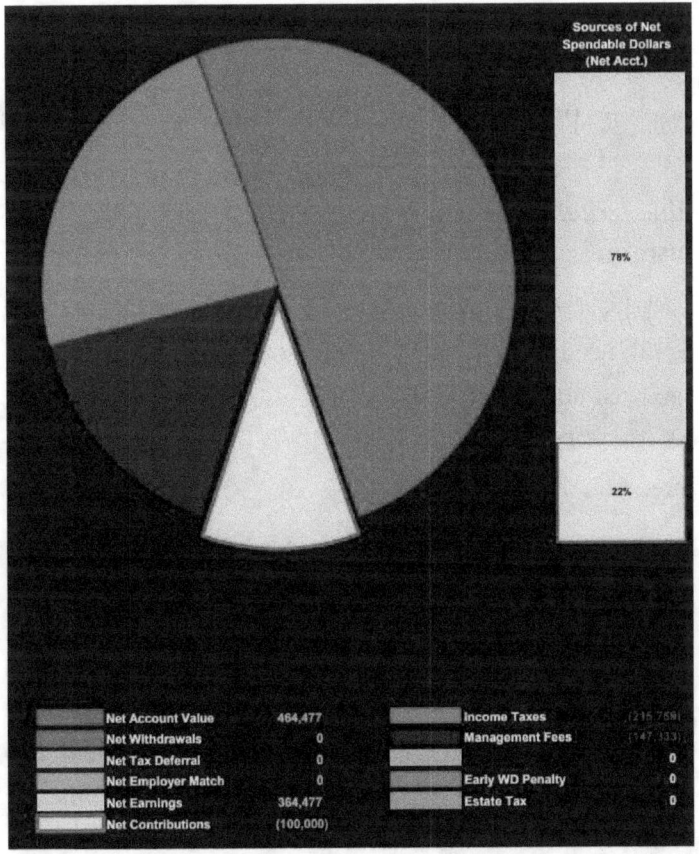

Want to see how we got these numbers? And what happens over a more extended time with distributions? Go to our book bonus materials: https://go.surewealthway.com/bonus to watch the video under **"Qualified plan."**

It is true: putting pre-tax dollars into a qualified plan gives you more money growing at the start. Then again, there's also more for planners and managers to constantly skim fees.

And, of course, the government will get its share too. However, you're running the unnecessary risk of higher taxes in the future. (Tax history charts are available as part of our book bonus:
https://go.surewealthway.com/bonus Look for **"Tax history."**)

Clearly, trading $20k (deferral) of "tax savings" for a $215k tax bill is a terrible trade-off. But this is "typical financial advice" at its finest. It's also worth asking: will it be easier to pay taxes now when you are working or after you have retired?

Deferring taxes also creates a false sense of security. Growing a retirement account with deferred taxes can psychologically fool you into thinking you have more than you really do. Yet a good portion of your retirement account isn't "your" money. As you can see, you'll also pay a fortune to the government and another fortune for plan fees and/or commissions.

As the calculator demonstrates, you may pay more in taxes and more in management fees than the out-of-pocket amount you put into the plan. Are you starting to understand why Wall Street and the government want you to max out your 401(k)?

Paying such bloated fees is common because compound interest doesn't just grow money, it also grows costs.

John Bogle, the founder of Vanguard, called this the "tyranny of compounding costs," the results are mind-boggling. It's no wonder Wall Street corporations spend billions lobbying the Department of Labor for industry-friendly policies that hand your money to them.

Your account, their rules. Even though it's "your" money, you can't use it while others profit from it. You must follow your employer's and the government's rules on what you can—and can't—do with your money.

If you want to use retirement funds to purchase a second home or to start a business, you'll encounter rules and roadblocks. Your retirement account is "statement wealth"—not usable wealth.

You can borrow money for specific limited purposes as long as you pay it back according to "the rules." For instance, IRA monies must be repaid within 60 days.

You'll often pay penalties and taxes if you withdraw retirement funds early. (There are exceptions, such as using IRA funds for a down payment on a home.) And be aware that you'll give up the gains that money could have earned. (The interest your money could have earned is your "opportunity cost," a key concept.)

The SureWealth philosophy takes opportunity costs into account. It also encourages people to take control of their money, so it benefits them first and foremost, not financial corporations or the government.

Additionally, you'll get hit the hardest if you have to withdraw money in a down market. Understanding how to diversify investments and sequence your disbursements in retirement can give you far more spendable retirement income. It may even put an six extra figures in your wallet–perhaps more. (Look for further information on the "Volatility buffer," as part of our Book bonus materials. https://go.surewealthway.com/bonus

The Target-Date Disaster

The most popular vehicle for a 401(k) and other qualified plans has become target-date funds, also called life-cycle funds. Overwhelmed with endless choices for mutual funds, investors and employers love the idea of set-it-and-forget-it simplicity: "Just pick the year you want to retire and sit back and relax!"

It sounds so attractive: a professionally managed fund that periodically reallocates money to lower investment risk as retirement approaches. Instead of manually making continuous adjustments to your portfolio to reduce stock market risk as the years progress, a target date fund purports to adjust automatically.

What could possibly go wrong?

Then the market crashed in 2008. Participants in the 2010 retirement funds—people who intended to retire around 2010—lost substantial percentages. In some cases, target-date funds dropped even more than the S&P 500.

Target-date funds were supposed to provide a safe retirement landing, but by 2010 target-date parachutes were failing to open. Many target-date funds were still in the stock market even as retirement dates approached—or passed. They failed to protect retirement funds from loss. (Unfortunately, strategies have not changed. The result will likely be the same in the next stock market crash.)

There are other issues with the funds as well. Performance has been lackluster at best and disastrous at worst. Their predetermined, formulaic design doesn't allow for reallocations in response to market conditions. And fees are high. Many "funds within a fund," have "fees upon fees."

And ironically, while target-date funds aim to simplify investment decisions, they're quite confusing.

Without analyzing pages of fine print, there's no way to know what's in the fund. Target-date funds with the same target year from different companies can vary wildly, creating a "buyer beware" situation for a product that, unfortunately, continues to sell itself.

We agree that investing doesn't have to be complicated, but target-date funds are not the solution. The SureWealth philosophy utilizes many financial vehicles that can be as simple as set-it-and-forget-it and without market risk.

Whatever Happened to Saving?

Typical financial advice often downplays saving in favor of investing. This worldview generates "assets under management" (and ever-renewing fees) for advisors and planners. While money managers may ask if you have an emergency fund, the more cash under your control, the less the money manager earns. As a result, building liquidity gets little more than lip service.

Many Americans think they are "saving" in their 401(k), but they don't have money when needed since it's designed to make access difficult. Nevertheless, over half of Americans have raided their retirement accounts early. Nearly one in four did so to pay off debt.[4] People are draining their retirement accounts to pay mortgages, college tuition, and credit card payments.

---

[4] https://www.cnbc.com/2019/09/05/half-of-americans-have-raided-their-retirement-savings-early.html

Savings and investing are both significant. Saving, not investing, builds your financial foundation.

Proper saving gives you stability and flexibility. Saving enables you to invest *without* liquidating your investments whenever a financial emergency arises. But saving isn't just for emergency funds. Saving is an essential life-long habit that provides liquidity to your life and business.

The SureWealth philosophy teaches people to save before (and during) investing. We recommend saving for "opportunities" as well as emergencies. We also teach you to measure opportunity costs before paying cash for major purchases. (There is often a better, more efficient use for your dollars.)

But where can you save safely where your money can keep up with inflation? The low-interest rate environment has turned accumulated wealth into mere trickles of income. These days, even multi-millionaires cannot live off interest generated by bank savings accounts and certificates of deposit.

The SureWealthWay utilizes a safe, reliable, tax-advantaged cash alternative with multiple benefits and tremendous flexibility. As a long-term savings strategy, it generates stronger returns than bank accounts, CDs, money market funds, fixed annuities, or treasury bills.

If you already have substantial savings, we utilize **private lending cash flow vehicles,** paying regular monthly payments. These strategies can generate healthy returns in the mid-to-high single digits and do not have a roller-coaster ride with the stock market.

Bank INsecurity

Speaking of saving money, everyone assumes the safest place for your money is an FDIC-insured account. Meanwhile, the Federal Reserve only has the equivalent of about 2% of the nation's bank deposits in their reserves. If there were ever a run on the banks, there currently wouldn't be money left to pay all the depositors. It would highlight just how much our fractional-reserve banking system is one enormous Ponzi scheme.

However, the financial system doesn't have to collapse for you to lose savings. Cyber-crimes and fraud strip money from bank accounts each year at a rapidly increasing pace. Government agencies such as the IRS and local law enforcement regularly confiscate funds from bank accounts.

Inflation is the most likely suspect robbing your bank account. At current interest and inflation rates, having "money in the bank" guarantees your wealth will quickly erode.

SureWealth strategies utilize an alternative to the Big Banks to store and grow cash. For those relying on interest payments, we suggest CD alternatives that can generate substantial cash flow inside or outside an IRA.

The sad truth is that much of the financial industry sells Americans a path to Wealth, leading them in the wrong direction.

Our "investments" have brought us great insecurity and the inability to plan for Anything. The inducements to stop working at age 65 have also betrayed those who can't make the numbers work. And too often, those advising us profit from keeping our dollars at risk.

We have less stability, control, or real prosperity than ever before. And that's why we assert:

"Typical" financial planning and advice is insane.

So, where did it all go wrong?

How did we get into this mess? Buckle your seatbelt; we're about to show you.

And more importantly:

What can you do to escape the insanity?

CHAPTER 3

How Did We Get Here?

Many wealthy people have always practiced what we now call the "SureWealth philosophy." Therefore, studying how people built wealth before the financial planning industry can help us discern what went wrong.

Before the rise of the financial planning industry in the 1970s, the most-used strategies were "savings accounts, whole life insurance, and the home mortgage," said Steve Utkus, director of the Vanguard Center for Retirement Research, quoted in the book "Pound Foolish."

Were Americans more financially savvy then? They didn't need to be because the typical family's finances –and financial products—were less complicated.

Nobody needed to know the difference between index and exchange-traded, hedge, and target-date funds. And nobody needed to understand the dangers of derivatives, credit-default swaps, and collateralized debt obligations.

Stock brokerage accounts were primarily for the upper-middle class and the wealthy— those who could afford to take some risks with their money. The average person did not yet have the sort of "easy and automatic" access to the stock market and mutual fund investing that exists today.

People tracked their savings instead of their credit card debt. Over time, homes turned into free-and-clear assets. Today, homes are used as collateral to refinance credit cards.

The number one fear was public speaking, not running out of money.

Life insurance provided financial security for widows, widowers, and other heirs left behind. The great majority of policies included lifelong savings in addition to protection.

In 1976, a majority of policies issued were permanent whole-life policies that built "cash value." Permanent life insurance didn't just replace income in the event of death; many average people used these policies to replace a leaky roof, fund a business, provide income for retirees and get families through a medical crisis.

Today, typical financial advice says to purchase life insurance until your kids grow up—then says to get rid of it right before you need it the most!

This radical shift from "permanent" to "temporary" term insurance (which can fill a need for affordable protection) is part of a larger shift in savings habits and the overall liquidity of U.S. households.

Personal savings rates rose to a temporary peak of 14% in 1975 and bottomed out post-2000 at about 2%. Pandemic restrictions and stimulus checks increased savings momentarily in 2020 and 2021.

Yet, the savings rate has already settled again to only 3.5 percent—a fraction of what people used to save.

Americans still spend more of their income and save less than earlier generations. The next chart illustrates the U.S. savings rate from 1960 through August 2022. Americans are currently saving just above the all-time lows preceding the Great Recession.

United States Personal Savings Rate

Today, the decline in savings is a major financial challenge. Debt has become the

Norm, not saving. Fortunately, saving money is something that we can control. It may take work. Saving takes budgeting, discipline, a change of priorities, and a change of habits. ***But saving is possible!***

Longevity has also been a trend. Again, there's good news here, considering the Alternative. When combined with the trend of retirement at 65, longevity becomes, in the language of mutual fund managers, a "risk."

Typical financial advice tells us that chasing high stock market returns is the solution to low savings rates and longevity. But this advice has only created financial insecurity.

Two other factors that have changed the face of the American economy are the advent of Social Security and the rise—and fall—of pension plans.

Before the Depression and the Social Security Act of 1935, there was no "retirement." Social Security was introduced to incentivize older workers to give up their jobs to younger workers—and it worked. Soon, companies followed suit by encouraging and mandating retirement at various ages.

Thus began the "safety net" and a set of cultural expectations that, along with increased life expectancies, has evolved into an unsustainable situation.

Between 1945 and 1965, worker-to-beneficiary ratios decreased from 41 workers per Social Security beneficiary to only four workers per beneficiary. Today, only 2.8 workers per retiree exist—and the ratio is expected to drop to as few as ***two workers per beneficiary*** by 2030.[5]

Simultaneously, defined-benefit pension plans have become financially unsustainable for corporations that once embraced them. Pensions were once considered necessary to attract quality employees. However, as retirees

[5] https://www.mercatus.org/publications/social-security/how-many-workers-support-one-social-security- retiree

lived longer and corporations fought to control costs, pensions began to fail. They suffered from the same magic-market thinking as 401(k)s, relying on risk and luck to meet obligations.

Today, defined benefit pension plans have been replaced with defined contribution plans such as 401(k)s. The move to defined contribution has shifted most or all of the responsibility of retirement savings onto employees.

Whether the mechanism is Social Security, pension plans, or individual retirement accounts, retiree financial woes stem from the assumption that everybody can retire at 65 and the numbers will somehow all work themselves out.

Of course, some people can afford to retire at 65 or younger with plenty of income for lifestyle. But is that the best outcome? Many people are better off—financially and otherwise—when they discover what they love to do and find a way to do *that* for a living for as long as they can.

Ultimately, our strained Social Security system and the fall of pensions are only a fraction of "what went wrong" in the economic story. While many events have impacted our financial system, let's take a quick tour of some of the highlights and lowlights of the economic timeline of the United States.

Signposts of a Financial Train Wreck

#1. Prior to 1913: Booms and busts, bank failures, and stock market crashes were the norms. At the time, market crashes only impacted the rich and the foolish.

#2. 1913: The Federal Reserve was created, putting our country's monetary policy in the hands of private bankers.

#3. September 3, 1929, marked the stock market high before the long slide into the Great Depression.

#4. 1935: The Social Security Act is passed to get older workers to leave their jobs to younger workers.

#5. November 23, 1954: The Dow finally regains its September 3, 1929 high.

#6. The 1950s: "financial planning" consists of a savings account, a life insurance policy, and home ownership. America enjoys a period of prosperity.

#7. 1958: The American Express card and BankAmericard (which became Visa in 1976) are introduced but not widely used or accepted until the 1980s.

#8. Late 1960s-early 1980s: Personal savings rates average 8-12% per year.

#9. In 1971, under Richard Nixon, the government moves away from the gold standard (backing the dollar with gold). The door is open to money printing and inflation.

#10. 1970s: The money supply more than doubles in the next decade, causing record inflation as more dollars chase the same goods and services. Inflation skyrockets the price of imported goods, such as oil. The ***Wall Street Journal*** reflects in January 1986, saying, "OPEC got all the credit for what the U.S. had mainly done to itself."

#11. 1972: IAFP enrolls its first group of students for the Certified Financial Planners (CFP) course at the College for Financial Planning.

#12. 1978: The section of the Internal Revenue Code that made 401(k) plans possible is enacted into law. It is intended to allow taxpayers a break on taxes on deferred income. However, in 1980, benefits consultant Ted Benna takes note of the previously obscure provision and figures out how to use it to save for retirement.

#13. By 1980, pension plans cover nearly 36 million private-sector workers, both union and non-union.

#14. 1980s: Fueled by demand created by the rise of qualified plans, the mutual fund industry explodes, lowering the barrier of entry to the stock market.

#15. 1980s-early 1990s: Deregulation opens the door to the massive Savings & Loan Crisis, which costs taxpayers upwards of $124 billion.

#16. 1980s & 1990s: As 401(k) and qualified plans rise in popularity, the masses begin to invest in the stock market. "Financial education" programs begin to teach and encourage employees how to "invest" (or speculate) in the stock market.

#17. Late 1980s and beyond: Many defined benefit pension plans become defined contribution plans. The risk and responsibility for retirement savings gradually shift from employer to employee.

#18. Late 1980s and beyond: Saving less and less, Americans shift from being "savers" to "investors," seeking higher and higher rates of return on their investments.

#19. 1980s: A.L. Williams popularizes the concept "buy term and invest the difference." Williams founds a company that rakes in billions selling pricey term insurance and high-fee mutual funds.

#20. 1980s and beyond: Mutual fund fees and "assets under management" create unprecedented profits for financial

corporations and a massive drain on retirement funds. Americans shift their savings from bank accounts, CDs, and insurance policy cash value accounts to "securities."

#21. Until 1986, credit card interest is tax-deductible, fueling the rapid rise of the credit industry and further lowering the savings rate.

#22. 1980s and beyond: Chasing higher returns, more and more Americans cash in their life insurance policies and go into old age with no life insurance. The middle class loses a primary mechanism for transferring wealth to heirs. The Monopoly board card that says, "Collect $100, your life insurance endows," becomes nonsensical to younger Americans.

#23. 1990s and beyond: Credit card companies change the way Americans spend. Now a middle or working-class American could "have it all!" Savings rates plummet to a mere 2%. People spend more and save less in attempts to have it all now.

#24. Late 1990s and beyond: Target-date funds gain popularity with increasing speed as more Americans hand over the responsibility for their financial futures to Wall Street corporations.

#25. Early 2000s: Deregulation, speculation, new accounting practices, executive spending, and company crimes create massive corporate meltdowns, such as Enron (2001) and Worldcom (2002). The stock market strays further from being a vehicle for investing in companies looking for capital and more about gaming a system where the big winners are few. Market investors get skimmed on a good day and outright swindled on a bad one.

#26. December 2007: After 14 months of heavy lobbying of Congress, the Pension Protection Act authorizes employers to place employees' qualified plan savings in **target-date funds as a "default" option** if an employee does not choose otherwise. Target-date funds are usually comprised mostly of stocks, and they replace stable value funds (generally regarded as a safe, conservative fund designed to protect the principal) as a default option.

#27. The same Pension Protection Act also establishes a "**safe harbor**" for **employers who automatically enroll** employees into 401(k) plans, ensuring they won't be liable for losses as long as they place their employees' money into target-date funds, managed funds, or balanced funds (all typically stock market securities.)

Can we pause here to ponder the absurdity of this legislation? Employers cannot be liable if they place an employee's money in investments that lose money in the stock market. And employers enjoy this safe harbor protection only if they place their employees' money in risky investments! And this is called the "Pension Protection Act?" It sounds more like the "Wall Street Commission and Bonus Protection Act."

#28. 2008-2009: One year after those changes occurred, American investors sustained considerable losses in the biggest stock market crash since the Great Depression. Neither the lawmakers, brokers, money managers, the Department of Labor, nor the employers were liable for losses.

#29. 2007-2010: The subprime mortgage crisis also causes deep homeowner and investor losses in real estate. The average American household loses **one-third of its net worth** as the value of both homes and stocks plummet.[6] The subprime mortgage crisis and recession create a national wave of foreclosures.

#30. 2007-2008: Two Goldman Sachs traders initially turn the crisis into large profits for the firm; they **earn $4 billion "betting" on a collapse in the sub-prime market** while **short-selling mortgage-backed securities**. Goldman CEO and Chairman Lloyd Blankfein oversees Goldman's risky bets on the housing bubble, then turns the investment firm into a bank so it could get TARP money.

---

[6] https://www.smithsonianmag.com/smart-news/average-american-household-lost-third-their-net-worth- during-recession-1809521

#31. 2008: Wall Street executives receive golden parachutes for a luxurious living while losing Main Street savings and investments. **The Big Banks take $175 billion in taxpayer bailouts while paying out $32.6 billion in bonuses to CEOs and key employees.** Not wanting to appear greedy, Blankfein forgoes his 2008 bonus, not wanting to appear greedy, but still rakes in $42.9 million in salary, stock options, and other compensation.

#32. December 2008: Interest rates hit an all-time low and stay there for years, turning accumulated nest eggs into mere trickles of income.

#33. March 5, 2009: The Dow Jones falls to its low of 6,594.44, less than 50% of its all-time high less than 18 months earlier.

#34. 2009 and beyond: As unemployment remains high, record numbers of people begin collecting Social Security at 62 because they cannot find work to meet their expenses.

#35. 2011: New census numbers considering rising healthcare costs reveal that one in six Americans 65 and older live in poverty. In the U.S., seniors have lost more economic ground than any other age group. Medicaid costs increasingly strain state and federal budgets.

#36. At one time, 88% of private sector companies with retirement plans provided employee pension plans.[7] By 2011, 97% had either discontinued defined benefit pensions or watered them down, combining them with defined contribution plans.

#37. April 2012: The first U.S. public pension plan declares bankruptcy.[8] Underfunded private and public pensions become increasingly invested in the stock market and begin to fail with greater frequency and impact.

#38. 2012: The "Retirement Savings Drain Report" discovers that management fees drain 31% or more of the average retirement fund. A real number of often six-figure losses to fees by the time a typical investor enters retirement.[9] (Fees drain additional profits during retirement.)

#39. 2011-2014: Americans continue to invest in the stock market, which crashed only a few years ago, even as it becomes increasingly unstable with speed trading and other technologies. Target-date funds continue to grow in popularity despite risks and (often) hidden and layered fees.

---

[7] https://protectpensions.org/2016/08/04/happened-private-sector-pensions/
[8] https://www.investmentnews.com/in-an-apparent-first-a-public-pension-plan-files-for-bankruptcy-43685
[9] https://www.demos.org/research/retirement-savings-drain-hidden-excessive-costs-401ks

(It's worth noting that many financial professionals are not fans of these funds, but for newbie investors, target-date funds and "robo-advisors" begin to replace professional advice.)

#40. 2013: Americans watch their mutual funds bounce back to pre-recession levels. They start using credit again, and spending increases. It is declared a "recovery."

#41. 2012 - 2021: While the stock market rebounds in an impressive bull run, rumors circulate of the "education bubble," the "bond bubble," the "everything bubble," and other financial accidents waiting to happen.

#42. 2017: Many seniors live under financial restrictions and uncertainty. While official poverty numbers are lower, 15 million people ages 65 and older (30.1%) have incomes below 200% of the poverty threshold, or $23,512 in 2017.[10]

#43. 2020: Year one of the coronavirus pandemic and restrictions. Small businesses and entire economies are knee-capped as big box stores and tech companies flourish. Many workers discover they can earn *more* on temporarily fortified unemployment benefits, creating further challenges for small business owners who struggle to find staff.

---

[10] https://www.kff.org/report-section/how-many-seniors-live-in-poverty-issue-brief/

#44. 2020: The stock market experiences its fastest crash ever in March 2020. Some investors sell their stocks just before the Fed starts pumping cash into the economy, using market manipulation to stop the pain. $3 trillion fuels a historic stock market rebound and other excesses.[11]

#46.[12] 2021: Unprepared for financial disruptions, a stunning half of Americans with retirement accounts (51%) admit to early withdrawals before and during the pandemic response.[13]

#47. 2021: As more banking transactions go online, fraud and losses increase dramatically. As we explain in our new special report, "Why Your Bank Account Isn't as Safe as You Think," banks are becoming one of the worst places to store your money!

#48. 2022: Fueled by money printing, inflation hits a four-decade high. Official estimates of approximately 9% inflation fail to reflect record-high gas, grocery, and housing prices adequately. Families struggle to pay for the basics. Ray Dalio says that his concern about inflation has jumped to "between an eight and a ten on a scale of one to ten."

---

[11] https://www.nasdaq.com/articles/graphic-federal-reserves-%243-trillion-virus-rescue-inflates-market- bubbles-2020-07-13
[12] https://jacobin.com/2021/12/house-speaker-paul-stocks-insider-trading-wealth
[13] https://www.cnbc.com/2021/11/22/half-of-americans-with-retirement-accounts-have-taken-early- withdrawals.html

#49. 2022: Oxfam releases a report revealing that the wealthiest billionaires "had a terrific pandemic." The ten richest individuals worldwide have doubled their collective wealth since 2020, adding 1.2 billion dollars per day during the pandemic. Meanwhile, incomes fell for almost everyone else. Over 160 million people were impoverished.[14]

#50. 2022: Interest rates are rising, which typically brings down asset prices. In June 2022, Forbes reports, "New Construction Plummets,"[15] and warns that a falling housing market could "torpedo the economy."[16]

Justin Haskins of The Federalist announces, "A shockingly large price bubble appears to have formed in the real estate market." Citing the impact of the ultra-low 2021 rates on the market, Haskins observes, "Americans have never seen housing prices skyrocket like they are now for this long of a period," adding, "If the current real estate bubble pops soon... it could end up being the largest real estate crash in history."[17]

---

[14] https://www.commondreams.org/news/2022/01/17/billionaires-had-terrific-pandemic-while-inequality-killed- millions-oxfam

[15] https://www.forbes.com/sites/jonathanponciano/2022/06/16/housing-market-in-free-fall-as-new- construction-plummets-heres-when-reset-could-cool-prices/?sh=41d398ef3a9e

[16] https://www.forbes.com/sites/sergeiklebnikov/2022/06/15/mortgages-surge-past-6-and-hit-their- highest-level-since-2008-housing-market-could-torpedo-us-economy-expert-warns/?sh=6e95d90c3574

[17] https://thefederalist.com/2022/02/16/key-indicator-hints-america-is-headed-for-its-worst-real-estate-crash-in- history/

In August 2022, Moody's predicts major housing markets will fall 20% or more.[18]

#51. 2022: US GDP shrinks two quarters in a row—the very definition of a recession. Despite clear signposts, the White House attempts to redefine "recession." Besides negative economic growth, record-breaking inflation. and a housing market past the tipping point, there is record-breaking US corporate debt of 22.5 trillion[19] and a slowing jobs market. Tesla, Apple, and Microsoft begin pausing hiring or laying off workers. Those who predicted the 2008 crash expect that another perhaps worse financial meltdown is on the horizon.

Michael Burry of "The Big Short" fame is betting against this market and has been warning of runaway inflation for two years. He's also been tweeting ominous warnings. Recently, he suggested the "mother of all crashes" was already underway.

Ray Dalio: "Most people have no idea what is coming," said Dalio, of Bridgewater Associates, one of the world's largest hedge funds. Critical of central bank policy and well aware of "bubbles" in the markets, Dalio predicts a bleak picture for

---

[18] https://fortune.com/2022/08/24/housing-market-falling-home-prices-2023-downgraded-forecast- moodys-analytics/
[19] https://webtribunal.net/blog/us-corporate-debt/

both cash and stockholders and a 2022 financial crisis that will lead to a stock market crash.

Jamie Dimon: JP Morgan Chase CEO warned investors that extraordinary financial circumstances are creating a potential economic hurricane. "That hurricane is right out there, down the road, coming our way," he said. "We just don't know if it's a minor one or Superstorm Sandy or Andrew. You better brace yourself."

True to form, the financial media ignores the warning signs, censors the solutions, and analysts continue their never-ending game of speculating what the next hot stocks will be. Only financial experts not sponsored by financial corporations dare to suggest that stocks will not continue to rise forever.

Massive conflicts of interest have shaped the institutions, products, and financial education that influence how Americans invest. Any objective observer looking at the economic history of the United States will agree that trusting Wall Street corporations is not the way to financial security.

Typical financial advice is not the answer.

Regardless of what regulations are passed or repealed, big financial corporations will continue to make money from customers/investors, whether or not they make money for customers/investors.

Typical financial planning and advice still utilize a broken system of half-truths and mathematical shortcomings to help Americans create "financial security."

People continue to aim for retirement at 65—or even much earlier—despite the economic risks. Many companies and industries continue to encourage or even mandate retirement despite the experience and wisdom that seniors can contribute.

With the recent roller-coaster ride of the stock market, the once-thriving "FIRE" movement (Financial Independence, Retire Early, usually through aggressive saving and investing) has been declared "dead" on multiple blogs. Even FIRE pioneer Sam Dogen declared a new definition for FIRE: "Foolish Idealist Returns to Employer."

Is it time to change course and try something different?

Maybe instead of "buying the dip," it's time to exit the stock market.

Maybe it's time to create your OWN "pension plan."

Maybe it's time to stop speculating and ask, "Where can I find guarantees?"

Maybe it's time to protect yourself and your money using time-tested financial vehicles and strategies.

CHAPTER 4

The SureWealth Way

If typical financial planning doesn't work, what does?

We started observing what wealthy people did when we learned about the problems with typical financial advice and strategies.
We looked for patterns of thought and action. We noticed what habits and strategies the prosperous had in common. And we realized that those on their way to financial freedom did things differently.

Wealthy people weren't following "conventional wisdom" or the plan Wall Street had for them. Frequently, the successful business owners and entrepreneurs I met were not:

- Investing in the stock market

- Maxing out 401(k)s
- Pre-paying mortgages
- Saving in savings accounts and paying 1% interest
- Working traditional jobs until "retirement age"
- Deferring their income taxes until retirement
- Putting their income and future in someone else's control

Wealthy people don't follow "typical" financial plans. They don't max out their 401(k)s, cross their fingers and wait. They don't delegate all control to big financial corporations and the government.

Many wealthy people practice what I have come to call the "SureWealth philosophy and strategies."

Fortunately, you don't have to be a millionaire to adopt the same strategies (although you can be). It would help if you learned to think like a wealthy person. As Tony Robbins says, "Success leaves clues." Learn to think and act like a wealthy person, and you will become one.

SureWealth strategies seek to protect your principal as it grows rather than chase unreliable returns. (And some strategies produce solid returns as well.) Its strategies and products do not rely on guesses and assumptions, the political climate, the mood of the market, or government policy.

SureWealth teaches families and individuals to think more like businesses and less like a passive consumers. Instead of accumulating money in retirement accounts where it is ignored or results are unpredictable, dollars are put to work.

SureWealth recognizes that "planning" is of limited use because when does life ever go as planned? Life may be unpredictable, but your financial strategies don't have to be.

The SureWealth Way starts with wherever you are right now. Whether you feel like you're "behind" on your finances or have experienced great prosperity, it deals with your current money.

Rather than trying to predict the future, the focus is on optimizing your dollars, making them more efficient, and using what you have to its fullest potential.

The SureWealth Way puts you back in control of your money, using proven strategies that do not rely on luck, skill, speculation, or a bull market.

SureWealth uses proven, time-tested strategies and products.

We recommend alternative financial products and solutions to clients, allowing them to get results while protecting themselves from an unstable stock market and banking system.

We have alternative strategies for **cash, income, and growth** that we have used for over a decade with our clients. These strategies do not rely on speculation and are innoculated to market cycles and crashes.

With the SureWealth Way, everything is measured mathematically. We use financial calculators to confirm the results of both current and proposed strategies. If the numbers aren't verifiable, we won't move forward.

The SureWealth Way is a proven alternative to typical financial planning and advice. We use special financial software (Truth Concepts) to confirm that the numbers work— and they do. But this type of planning is about much more than math. It's a different way of doing things. It's not just changing a running shoe. It's transforming the runner's technique and conditioning so they reach their destination faster and more safely.

The SureWealth Way encompasses products (things that you buy) **and strategies** (things that you do). It's a flexible system that cannot be reduced to a single product or strategy.

The SureWealth philosophy is also about more than money. We believe true wealth is a way of thinking and of living, and it goes beyond dollars. It also includes health, happiness, and fulfillment when we live our purpose, dwell in gratitude, and do the right thing.

The Sure Wealth Way is a philosophy and a set of principles that inform your financial choices and puts you back in control of your thinking - and your money.

Let's look at the 10 Truths of the SureWealth Way. These principles make SureWealth what it is: a better, safer, more secure strategy for building wealth.

* * *

CHAPTER 4

The 10 Truths of the SureWealth Way

Although we have coined the term "SureWealth" and have articulated the 10 Truths of the SureWealth philosophy, the ideas and practices of SureWealth are not new.

We didn't invent the SureWealth Way; many wealthy people have practiced it for generations. We've observed and described the timeless principles and practices of wealth building.

We use the **10 Truths of the SureWealth Way** and test on calculators and real-world case studies to guide our financial decisions. Practicing **SureWealth** means acting under these 10 Principles:

Truth #1: Guarantees—not guesswork

While many forms of investing may involve some risk, most investors take too much risk unnecessarily. You can demand a guarantee. While there's nothing wrong with having some money in the stock market if you desire, we recommend building your **core financial foundation** in products that are guaranteed not to lose money.

Most people only have the opportunity to view projections from financial advisors and planners who depend exclusively on speculative, often optimistic market returns. SureWealth strategies are different because they rely on guarantees, not speculation.

The SureWealth Way allows you to count on your money when needed. You are guaranteed a minimum growth on your money (although you may earn more). SureWealth offers assurance that you will not lose your gains in volatile markets and geopolitical turmoil. And our life insurance strategies guarantee you can never outlive your policy.

Truth #2: Cash flow beats paper profits.

Typical financial planning focuses on building the largest portfolio possible—a portfolio in a retirement account you can't use and don't control for most of your life.

You can't buy groceries with paper profits—and having a big portfolio you can't touch while stressing about expenses is no use. When interest rates head toward zero (as they have done multiple times since 2008), you'll want to have the cash flow you need without liquidating your principal.

While the goal of much financial planning appears to just be to build a secure retirement for the advisor with assets under management, SureWealth strategies create usable wealth and cash flow for the saver/investor.

There also are psychological benefits to this approach. Instead of worrying whether or not you can "turn on the tap" when you retire, you'll be practicing creating income along the way. Building cash flow gives you confidence in your financial strategies. SureWealth strategies also free up your time and energy. You can give up tracking the stock market's moves and enjoy your life.

Truth #3: Keep control of your cash

Having timely access to cash when you need it is called liquidity. It's the opposite of having money "tied up" where you can't get to, use, or borrow against it.

Liquidity brings control, and control brings security. When you have access to cash—or the ability to collateralize assets—you can handle emergencies without cashing out your portfolio.

Many people discovered the importance of control and liquidity during the Great Recession. Their 401(k)s became 201(k)s when investors sold their positions for a loss, either because they panicked or needed the money. Unfortunately, they also likely paid taxes, fees, and penalties.

But cash isn't just for emergencies; It's also for opportunities. When you find a fantastic real estate deal or another financial opportunity, you want to be able to take advantage of it. SureWealth keeps your cash growing while giving you access to capital when needed.

Truth #4: Keep interest compounding for you

Einstein declared, "Compound interest is the eighth wonder of the world. Those who understand it earn it. Those who don't pay it." Compound interest is a powerful force that you want working for you rather than against you.

When you are earning interest, the growth curve accelerates over time. Your gains have gains, interest earns interest, and growth gains momentum.

To work with compound interest, keep saving and investing. Consistency is the key. Avoiding disruptions is the secret to keeping the growth curve growing. Avoid high-interest debt and recurring fees to keep compounding from working against you.

When you pay interest, the costs—not the interest—compound. Would you love to earn 18, 19, or even 22% on your money? One way is to avoid getting trapped in high-interest credit card business debt. (Most people think this means always paying cash, but as you'll see in Principle #7, there may be better options.)

Even when investing, compounding costs work against you. Those "little" fees add up big-time over the years. Vanguard founder Jack Bogle called it "the tyranny of compounding costs," which can cost you a fortune. The average American family loses six figures, sometimes multiple six figures, to those tricky recurring fees and commissions.

The younger you are, the more you will lose to compounding fees. NerdWallet demonstrated that paying just 1% in fees could cost a saver/investor $590,000 in returns over 40 years.[20]

Truth #5: Minimize or eliminate taxes

Taxes are often a person's most signifcant expense. In 2021, a study by Self revealed that the average American pays more than $525,000 in taxes over a lifetime.[21] Nearly two-thirds of that represents income tax. So, one secret to more money is keeping Uncle Sam out of your pocket.

Typical financial advice encourages people to max out their 401(k)s, partly for the tax advantages. Yet this short-sighted

---

[20] https://www.nerdwallet.com/blog/investing/millennial-retirement-fees-one-percent-half-million-savings- impact/
[21] https://www.thefiscaltimes.com/2021/05/17/Average-American-Will-Pay-525000-Taxes-Over-Their-Lifetime-Study

strategy does little to reduce taxes; it only defers them. It is too late; many people discover it is more difficult to pay income taxes after they leave their jobs in retirement. And with recent government spending sprees, do you think taxes are going up or down?

The SureWealth Way doesn't kick the "tax can" down the road. We teach clients to move money from "forever taxable" environments to never taxable. You can do this in many ways, such as:

- Utilize Roth IRAs, especially self-directed IRAs
- Operate a business (even a side hustle) to increase tax deductions. Use dividend-paying whole-life insurance for your long-term savings.
- Save and grow cash in financial vehicles that protect you from taxation.
- Take advantage of real-estate-related tax deductions for homes and rentals.
- Use temporary loans instead of permanent withdrawals from tax-advantaged environments.

Truth #6: Opportunity costs lead to loss

Typical advice will tell you to pay for major expenses with cash. But is that the best strategy? Contrary to what the financial industry wants you to believe, you might lose more than you gain because paying cash has a cost—paying with cash costs you the dollars you could have earned by investing that money!

Financial calculators demonstrate it makes no sense to pay cash to avoid a 2.9% car loan when those dollars could earn 4, 6, or perhaps even 8 percent with other strategies.

Consider opportunity costs in all financial decisions. Remember the story of the golden goose? Keep your golden goose (your principal) alive, well, and growing. Take care of the goose, and it will take care of you. Feed the goose and pay expenses with the eggs. This truth keeps the foundation of your wealth safe, growing, and liquid.

Truth #7: Give your money multiple jobs

If you want your dollars to work harder, give them more than one job to do. Don't settle for "lazy assets." Money works harder when it does multiple jobs, such as creating wealth and giving benefits simultaneously.

A dollar in a savings account does one thing. It pays a little bit of interest, thus creating a tiny growth. Otherwise, it's a lot like putting your money under a mattress.

In contrast, a dollar in our favorite alternative savings vehicle (a dividend-paying mutual life insurance policy structured for maximum legal cash value per IRS guidelines) can do some or all of the following:

- Grow faster over time than a savings account
- Create a tax advantage (Done correctly, you'll never pay tax on the growth)
- Pay a dividend (not guaranteed, but historically reliable for 160+ years)
- Build cash that can be used for collateral and easily borrowed against
- Create a growing death benefit as well as living benefits
- Protect money from creditors and predators with far greater privacy than a bank account (Protections vary by state)

Another way to make money work harder is to move dollars "through" assets, not just "to" assets. You can store cash in a life insurance policy and then borrow against the cash to invest in real estate or other opportunities. You can also move money through income assets (such as rental real estate or a mortgage note) and use the cash flow to purchase additional income-producing assets.

This cash flow strategy is one we love. It has a multiplying effect, increasing your money's "velocity," or speed.

Truth #8: Prepare for any possibility

To be truly prepared, you should forecast the good and bad possibilities and guard against disruptions. Interruption of work? Illness? Death or disability?

Outliving your money? These aren't pleasant things to think about, but thorough preparation will give you greater peace of mind.

We take our clients through a financial forecasting process. Whether you work with us or not, we believe it's essential to understand where you are financially. We take the actual numbers of your specific situation and show you how customized strategies can remove the guesswork of successfully navigating life's uncertainties.

We also recommend "self-completing" strategies that ensure your family can enjoy financial security whether you live to age 105, die young, or become disabled. You deserve the ability to remain in control even when the rest of the world or your circumstances are in doubt.

Truth #9: Envision your ideal outcome

While we love helping clients plan and prepare for uncertainty, your daily focus should not be on the scary "what ifs." Instead, envision the life you **want** for yourself and your family.

What if things work out precisely the way you want—or better? What if you become the person you dream of being? What if you travel to the destinations calling to your soul and make the difference you wish to make?

You are the scriptwriter of your destiny. There is a saying, "Whatever you think about, you will bring about." Therefore, empower yourself to achieve your dream results. This practice will serve you in every area of life.

Peace of mind matters. Once your roadmap is in place, you won't need to constantly watch the stock market and worry about what the economy will do next. Instead, build your business or career. Stay healthy. Love your loved ones. Enjoy your life and make it rich!

Truth #10: Leave a legacy that lasts

Your legacy is how you will be remembered and what you will leave behind. Legacy is so much bigger than money. And, of course, legacy often includes money left to heirs and charities.

Your legacy is your lived values and beliefs. What are the principles and values you want your life to represent? What unique wisdom is yours to share?

In the realm of money, research shows that if you're going to leave a legacy that lasts, you must leave more than money. Money without wisdom will soon be gone. When you leave an inheritance, you must teach future generations to care for, manage, and multiply the money.

The SureWealth Way isn't just a temporary solution, and it isn't just for you today. It is something to teach and model to future generations. There are even multi-generational life insurance strategies that can create perpetual family legacies.

The Ten Truths of the SureWealth Way are the principles guiding our products, strategies, and decisions.

Our truths lead to choices that diverge from conventional financial advice. Each individual or family can uniquely shape these choices to suit their circumstances. In the next chapter, we'll give examples of how to apply the Ten Truths to various areas of personal finance.

If you want to see how the principles apply to your situation, it's easier to show you rather than explain them in a book. That's because every roadmap is personal to you or your family.

To schedule a no-cost, no-obligation discussion book here: https://go.surewealthway.com/schedule

We'll have a brief conversation to address your queries and gain a basic understanding of your situation. Together, we can then determine the best course of action.

We can provide a financial forecast using your actual numbers to show you your future results based on current strategies. Where are your current financial habits and strategies taking you? Using special Retirement Analyzer software, we'll show you. There's no guesswork, and it's all verifiable using your actual numbers.

For a financial forecast, you fill out the information on a confidential and secure platform. We then calculate your present financial forecast based on your current financial habits, strategies, products, etc. We can also illustrate your future financial position based on various scenarios, such as differing life expectancy, retiring at different ages, or changes in income, habits or health. The analysis provides a comprehensive financial preview of your life.

Lastly, if we find we can help you, we will compare your present financial forecast to potential solutions. For example, we might suggest ways to increase your net worth, cash flow, and the benefits available to you and your family—often with no additional out-of-pocket costs. We can all see the differences and mathematically verify the longterm impact of proposed changes. Then you can decide if the changes make sense.

We take an educational approach. We encourage you to ask questions. Invite your current advisors, lawyer, CFP or accountant. Everything is transparent. There's no "sales pitch" or pressure. We don't expect your business if we can't improve your financial situation.

To find out more and book a no-obligation call, visit https://surewealthllc.com

or call 1-913-372-3032

Now let's look at some examples of what the SureWealth Truths and strategies look like in practice.

CHAPTER 5

SureWealth in Action

The **10 Truths** guide our decisions and lead us away from typical financial strategies and advice. Let's apply Sure Wealth thinking to real-world financial scenarios so you can see the difference.

Let's look at five specific examples of the SureWealth Way in action:

- Creating income/cash flow from assets
- Real estate
- Saving money
- Investing for growth
- Paying for college education

See how these areas can lead us to new thinking and greater efficiency and use of assets.

Example #1: Creating income/cash flow from assets

Typical financial advice follows the "accumulate now, withdraw later" plan. The problem with this is that people live on cash flow, not on net worth. Plus, typical income financial strategies won't keep pace with inflation.

Creating income or cash flow from assets is fundamental to any strategy for financial independence. Yet, most people are relying on strategies that ultimately handicap their cash flow, draining it with never-ending taxes and fees in retirement.

Typical financial advice leads to typical strategies (and typical problems):

- People are told to accumulate as much money as you can in your 401(k) and other retirement accounts until you start taking distributions. In the meantime, cross your fingers and pray the stock market doesn't crash.
- When people retire, they realize it will cost a fortune in income taxes to pull money out of a traditional retirement account. As a result, money remains in qualified plans where it continues to be taxed. Perhaps people roll over 401(k)s into IRAs, but (unless it is a Roth), they'll pay the same endless taxes.
- At or near retirement, stocks are often traded for less volatile, lower-risk assets. Hopefully, when it's your

time to retire, you can "sell high." If you retire when the market is depressed, should you wait for a recovery or cut your losses? (If that's you, ask us about a strategy that has benefitted many of our clients.)

- Advisors often say, "it will all work out," yet many people worry they will run out of money once retired. Even less volatile investments such as dividend stocks can lose substantial value and bonds that pay aggressively are often risky!
- People are told to draw down assets at no more than 3% of principal - or less. (The former "4% rule" has been downsized to a mere 2.25 to 2.5% due to high inflation. Withdraw faster, and you could deplete your nest egg.)
- Typically, you're advised to keep a portion of assets in cash equivalents such as certificates of deposit, although rock-bottom interest rates encourage many seniors to take unnecessary risks. And if you hold cash in your retirement account, you could be moving backwards after fees.
- Funds in taxable retirement accounts remain subject to future income taxes as well as various qualified plan rules. Most retirees resign themselves to pay income taxes forever at an unknown future income tax rate. (Given the recent explosion of government spending, many experts predict tax rates could soar.)

Looking at the uncertainties and disadvantages, we conclude that leaving your money in retirement accounts and withdrawing from it over decades is the best possible retirement plan for your financial planner or money manager!

Seriously, ask yourself if typical advice serves your best interests or someone else's. You take all the risk while they collect never-ending fees for "assets under management." We could say the same about Uncle Sam. You take all the risk while the government collects never-ending taxes.

And whether you are retired or not, there are multiple issues with certain income strategies:

- Earnings, if relying on dividends or bonds, are often low.
- Assets, if left in the market, may not hold value. What is an "acceptable" chance of loss or failure? How much risk can you take with your future?
- When money is left indefinitely in retirement accounts, taxation, commissions, and fees erode investments or cash flow.
- At some point in the market cycle, you'll likely be forced to liquidate stocks when they are comparatively "low." Are you mentally and financially prepared for the next 50%+ market crash?

- When you sell stock market assets in a down market, you never recover those losses. These losses have a devastating impact on your future income. (We can solve this with a tool called a "volatility buffer," which we explain further in this book's bonus materials. Look for **"Volatility buffer."**)
  https://go.surewealthway.com/bonus
- Required minimum distributions can increase taxes on your Social Security income. (Traditional planning is usually oblivious to issues with Social Security income, and problems often arise.)

The typical strategy could be more tax efficient. People tend to withdraw "a little at a time" from all available assets, which is rarely efficient. We look at which asset to draw from, when—and in what order. Most people are shocked to learn that the sequence, or order, withdraw or consume your assets makes a huge difference in your spendable income! You can sequence your assets to minimize taxation, put more money in your pocket, and reduce market risk.

Fortunately, there are ways to reduce income tax drastically if you make the right moves. When clients come to us with typical investments in taxable retirement accounts, we explore how to shift money from "forever taxable" financial vehicles to "never taxable" vehicles.

However, the biggest problem with typical strategies is that there's no reliable "fallback" plan for decreasing interest rates, increasing longevity, or major emergencies that could deplete assets.

No wonder seniors say their greatest fear is running out of money. The "accumulate now, draw down later" strategy relying on stocks and bonds is a poor plan with no emergency exit.

That's why we don't suggest using "typical strategies" when your goal is sustainable income.

Dividend stocks and REITs will rise and fall with the market. Other types of securities can be even more volatile. But there are investments and alternative strategies that offer the security of principal and healthy returns. Let's consider three:

- Real estate mortgage notes
- Guaranteed fixed -idexed annuities
- Reverse mortgages

Private lending vehicles such as carefully selected **real estate mortgage notes** can offer significant, reliable income. You'll want to work only with carefully screened and highly rated companies that offer fully collateralized notes with real-world assets.

There are many benefits of real estate mortgage notes that make this worth serious consideration for anyone who desires income:

- Being a private lender allows you to "be the bank" on a real estate deal rather than the buyer or seller. (This gives you the same protections and advantages other lenders have, including banks.)
- Private lenders receive reliable monthly income payments with contractual guarantees.
- Payments come directly from the real estate development company we recommend, not a renter.
- Assets can be secured with first-position mortgage instruments, depending on the amount. Loan-to-value ratios are conservative enough to allow for wide market fluctuations.
- Mortgage notes can be held in a self-directed Roth IRA for *tax-free income*.

Annuities can also provide steady income streams that you cannot outlive. If life insurance guards against dying too soon, annuities protect you from living too long and outlasting your nest egg.

Annuities are issued by life insurance companies and are available for anyone age 40 and over. Unlike life insurance, annuities do not require physical exams and are not "rated" according to health.

While fixed annuities are not paying well these days, guaranteed fixed-indexed annuities offer surprisingly generous income riders. These annuities can provide growth, income, and other benefits. For instance, optional riders can provide a death benefit or income for a surviving spouse or beneficiary.

Annuities are contractually guaranteed and offered by life insurance companies. However, they can be complex to understand. We can provide a spreadsheet comparison of dozens of annuities. This broad comparison helps identify the top five annuities. It highlights the various features to help clients explore their options and make informed decisions.

To understand how the proper annuity can help you generate guaranteed income in retirement, book a call today.

https://go.surewealthway.com/schedule

Last, you should know about a strategy that "saved the day" for a dear family member. A reverse mortgage can provide additional tax-free income when more money is needed than anticipated. Sometimes, it can even turn your mortgage payment into a payment you receive from the mortgage company. Additional income from illiquid assets can be a game-changer for homeowners under-saved for retirement.

Some important points to know about this strategy:

- Reverse mortgages allow seniors to "spend" home equity while remaining in their homes—with no mortgage payment. (Property taxes and insurance must be paid.)
- One of the significant financial advantages of reverse mortgages is that the income received does not impact social security income. This is because it is considered home equity, not income, and therefore, no income tax is owed on it.
- Combined with permanent life insurance, a reverse mortgage can provide income while keeping a (cash) inheritance in place. In some situations, heirs may choose to pay off the reverse mortgage and keep the home. Alternatively, they can receive any remaining home equity after selling the home.
- Reverse mortgages are not for everyone. Not every person or every property qualifies. (For starters, you must be age 62 or above with at least 50% equity in the home, which must be your primary residence.) In some situations, a different mortgage product (such as a home equity line of credit, or HELOC) may be more efficient.

Would you like some guidance? We can help you strategize a "big picture" solution involving two or more strategies discussed in this chapter and show you how they work together for greater synergy. Contact us at 1-913-372-3032 or info@surewealthllc.com

With typical strategies, people should be afraid of running out of money. We do not advocate leaving money in the stock market during retirement. Yet even target-date funds can expose nest eggs to the risk of loss after a person retires. With SureWealth strategies, you have greater flexibility and control.

Example #2: Real Estate

Typical financial advice (from Ms. Orman or Dave Ramsey) tells you:

- Save a 20% down payment
- Purchase a home with a 15-year mortgage if you can afford to do so
- Or get a 30-year mortgage and pay extra against the principal so you can pay off your home early and save on interest.
- In perhaps 15-20 years, you'll have a free and clear home. (Unless you refinance or sell the home to buy another, as many people do.)

On the surface, this makes sense. But is it the best option? Let's look at two different scenarios—paying off a mortgage early or selling one property to buy another—and see if there is a better way.

Your home is a significant asset—often your most prominent. And when you sign the escrow papers, you might get bug-eyed looking at the "Truth-in-Lending statement" that tells you how much interest you'll pay over 30 years.

For instance, you purchase a $500,000 home with a $400,000 mortgage at a 5% interest rate. Your principal and interest payment would be $2,147.29. (I'm excluding taxes and insurance for simplicity and using this calculator.) Over 30 years, you'd pay $773,023 for the mortgage, including $373,023 in interest.

Original Loan Amount	$400000		Payoff Amount: $400,000.00	
Original Loan Term	30	years	The remaining balance is $400,000.00. This is the amount required to repay the entire loan altogether. It will result in savings of **$373,023.14** in interest.	
Interest Rate	5	%		
Remaining Term	30	years	**The Original Payoff Schedule**	
	0	months	Monthly Pay	$2,147.29
			Total Payments	$773,023.14
			Total Interest	$373,023.14

Typical financial advice says, "Wow, that's a lot! You should reduce that interest!" So perhaps you pay a little extra each month. Let's say you pay an extra $300 each month, raising your monthly payment to $2,447.29.

At the same 5% interest rate, you'll pay off the mortgage seven years, one month early, reducing interest to $272,530 and saving $100,493! You congratulate yourself and feel confident that you saved over $100k. But did you consider opportunity costs?

Original Loan Amount	$400000
Original Loan Term	30 years
Interest Rate	5 %
Remaining Term	30 years
	0 months

Repayment Options:
○ Payback altogether
● Repayment with extra payments
$300 per month
$0 per year

Payoff in 22 years and 11 months

The remaining balance is $400,000.00. By paying extra $300.00 per month, the loan will be paid off in 22 years and 11 months. It is **7 years and 1 month earlier**. This results in savings of **$100,492.89** in interest.

If Pay Extra $300.00 per month

Monthly Pay	$2,447.29
Total Payments	$672,530.25
Total Interest	$272,530.25

The Original Payoff Schedule

Monthly Pay	$2,147.29
Total Payments	$773,023.14
Total Interest	$373,023.14

Truth #6 is, "Opportunity costs lead to loss." What's your opportunity cost if you had invested that $300/month elsewhere?

What if, instead of paying down your mortgage faster, you put that $300 a month somewhere else where it could have earned you 7% interest?

Many of our clients have steadily made 7 to 8% yearly on their money in private lending deals secured by real estate.

Perhaps you have a business where your investment return would be higher, but let's use 7%. How much would investing $300 per month yield at 7% over 22.08 years (the identical payment schedule)?

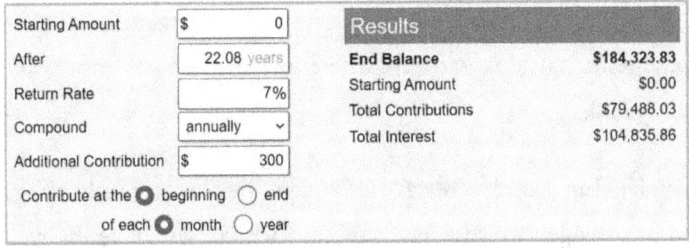

After 22 years, one month (the new/reduced loan term), the $300/month grows to $184,323. We've already received a positive benefit of $84,000! (Not to mention the peace of mind of a lower mortgage payment should you experience income disruptions or emergencies.) However, the original time frame that produced the $373,023 interest paid was 30 years. Let's keep that money invested through the entire 30 years to compare apples to apples.

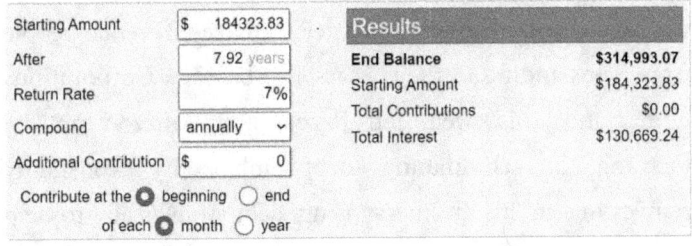

With no additional cash out of pocket, by leaving that money invested at $300/month at 7%, calculations show,[22] you would have $314,993. That recoups 84% of the interest on your 30-year mortgage, as the investment gains offset all but $58,030 of the mortgage costs.

---

[22] https://www.calculator.net/investment-calculator.html

The "invest elsewhere" strategy also beats the "extra payments" strategy toward the mortgage by an impressive $214,500.

By leaving your 30-year mortgage be (taking advantage of mortgage interest tax savings, which we haven't even mentioned) and putting $300/month to work elsewhere, you'll end up with a paid-off home plus $314,993 in your pocket. Isn't that what you'd rather have—nearly an additional $315k?

You can conceptualize opportunity cost by asking, "What else could I do with my dollars? Is there a better use for my money than eliminating a 5% interest rate? Could I earn more elsewhere?"

Do you see how typical financial advice prevents people from expanding their asset base? Corporations understand this well. Jeff Bezos built Amazon not by focusing on eliminating debt mbut by constantly reinvesting in his business using debt strategically to help him expand his assets and business.

That's the advantage of putting dollars to work. Paying extra toward your mortgage gives you some benefits. But spending money to expand your home equity is a lot like hiding money in the walls of your house! Home equity is a "lazy asset." It does not produce cash flow nor increase the value of your home.

When you think of your personal economy as a business you can make wise choices that lead to greater personal profits.

The Sure Wealth Way suggests a more efficient real estate strategy:

Buy a home when you can. Purchase a house when you can afford it, even utilizing opportunity to put down less that 20% if available. There is no need to wait to save the 20% while throwing years of extra rent payments down the drain—that is a wasted opportunity.

Get a 30-year mortgage with lower payments. Mortgage debt is typically low-interest and often tax-deductible. Keep monthly payments low and invest the difference elsewhere.

Put your dollars to work. Expand your asset base and increase your cash flow instead of focusing on paying off low-interest, tax-deductible debt.

Rather than building up your home equity, expand your asset base. Create assets you can use. You can never count on home equity. If market conditions or your income and credit situation change, your home equity may vanish or become inaccessible.

Saving and investing elsewhere increases your accessible, usable wealth.

And "investing on the side" isn't the only strategy; it's just the simplest. You can also increase your asset base and future cash flow by using equity to expand your real estate portfolio.

What is the result of utilizing such strategies? One client stopped renting and purchased her first home, "Property A," for $110k using a 3.5% down FHA loan. (This was several years ago.)

A few years later, she saved money for a down payment on her second home, "Property B," purchased for $200k. Instead of selling Property A, she turned it into a rental property.

A little over two years later, she sold Property A for a profit of about $90k. She used the tax-free proceeds (per current tax code) as a down payment on a new rental property, Property C, for $120k. (She also paid off her consumer debt, bought a car, and vacationed in Hawaii!)

Two years later, she refinanced her home, Property B, and used the proceeds as a down payment on a new home, Property D. Now she had two rental properties, Property B and Property C, plus a home.

Three years later, she sold the two rental homes—Property B and Property C—for a gain of over $200k. Much of that money was tax exempted since property B was her residence for two of the last five years. Plus, she still owned a home, Property D, that she could live in or offer for rent.

In 13 years, she had created windfalls totaling about $300k.

No "house flipping" or super risky strategies. Just smart moves to expand her asset base (and a healthy housing market).

At the time, she was a single mother earning about $60k per year in her "day job."

Could she have saved $300k from her salary in the same amount of time following typical financial advice? Probably not. But by SureWealth's thinking, she was able to expand her assets and make her money work harder.

She would have eventually paid off the loan if she had stayed in her first home and accelerated mortgage payments. Still, she would not have created the windfalls from additional properties.

Using SureWealth thinking, you can eventually have a free and clear home plus additional homes, investments, cash-flowing assets, and passive income.

Whether or not you are interested in being a landlord, expanding your asset base is a scalable strategy you can use in many areas of your personal economy.

Example #3: Saving Money

When people start saving, many use bank accounts or credit unions to build emergency funds. Others start putting their money into 401(k) plans and investments inside a qualified plan. Suppose your goal is growing savings with conventional strategies like these. In that case, you'll need to avoid the following problems and pitfalls:

- Banks currently pay perhaps 1.5% at this writing—if you shop for the most competitive rates—and that's taxable.
- A bank account is an "either/or" asset. You can put your dollar in the bank, but you'll have to take it out to access money for something else. In doing so, you interrupt the (modest) growth you earn on interest.
- Bank accounts are not necessarily private or secure. From cybercrimes, fraud, and identity theft to liens, lawsuits, and garnishments, there are countless examples of how someone's bank savings have ended up in someone else's pocket. (For more on this, download our special report, "Why Your Bank Account Isn't as Safe as You Think!")

- Money can be borrowed from a bank only if you "qualify" for the loan. If your credit or income situation changes for the worse, good luck!
- Qualified plans (i.e., 401(k), etc.) are poor vehicles for savings. These plans subject money to risk, restrict assets behind a cumbersome tax and penalty wall, and leave the cash inaccessible to savers.
- Investment and saving options are limited in qualified plans. Typically, your choices are to take risks with securities or park your money in a cash equivalent, earning next to nothing.
- Rules for borrowing from a retirement plan are strict and for limited purposes.

For instance, purchasing a franchise or buying a vacation home is disallowed. What if you urgently need money from your retirement account? Be prepared to pay hefty taxes and penalties.

The SureWealth solution is to save in a high cash value, dividend-paying whole-life policy structured with maximum paid-up additions. We say "save," not "invest," because most life insurance is not classified as an investment. Comparing cash value to safe, liquid vehicles and accounts that cannot lose value is more appropriate.

However, the benefits of utilizing a properly structured insurance vehicle far outweigh simple savings accounts and

CDs. It would be like comparing a battleship to a canoe. Both will get you across the ocean, but with vastly different levels of protection.

Using this strategy:

- When held long-term, internal rates of return are currently between 3-5% (depending on age and health). That's after the cost of insurance, commissions, and running the company.
- You'll have greater returns and more privacy and security than banks provide, with no stock market risk.
- Cash value is liquid, and you can borrow against it anytime for any reason. (Withdrawals are also allowed, but we don't recommend withdrawals in most situations when you can borrow against it tax and penalty-free.)
- The collateral strategy gives you consistent growth while allowing payment flexibility. Policyholders can repay policy loans on their schedule. At the same time, the cash value used as collateral keeps growing and is unaffected by loans.
- Cash value becomes "all-purpose" savings. Unlike a 529 IRA or HSA, you can use your savings for any purpose: home repairs, college tuition, rental property down payment, business expense, a wedding, or a new car.

- In many states, whole-life policy cash values are protected from liens, lawsuits, and (in all states) from the prying eyes of the Internal Revenue Service.
- Permanent insurance is an incredible protection strategy for couples and families. In a worst-case scenario, the payout ensures the well-being of a surviving spouse, partner, or child. This actuarial mechanism constantly grows the policyholder's estate and creates generational legacies.

Now, our topic here was saving, not life insurance. Few people think they "want" life insurance—until they understand the benefits! And when you consider the living benefits and opportunity costs, a life insurance policy becomes a superior savings vehicle compared to bank products. Consider the following:

- If you save in a qualified plan or a savings account and desire life insurance, you will have to pay additionally for term insurance that will end after a defined period (or face drastic premium increases).
- Term insurance premiums must be counted as an opportunity cost since you cannot save or invest elsewhere with those dollars. (Nor is your family likely to receive a death benefit since term life insurance almost always expires before you need it.)
- In certain situations, the policyholder can utilize death benefits while still living. For instance, policies

are assets that can be sold on the secondary insurance market. In terminal or chronic illness cases, accelerated death benefit options can (according to special riders) give the policyholder a cash injection.
- An adequately funded permanent insurance policy with the correct riders can reduce the need for some disability, term life, and even long-term care insurance. (Remember opportunity cost!)

Typical advice says, "Buy term and invest the difference." But, in practice, do people invest the rest or spend it? (From experience, we know that despite best intentions, they spend.) And if a family spends the difference, could that strategy leave a family under-protected in the future?

At the end of the term, term insurance comes to an end. Will you be ready to "self-insure," as some financial gurus suggest? And if not, what if your health has changed and you no longer qualify for life insurance?

Replacing a lifetime income is not easy. People who intend to self-insure often never reach the capability to actually do it. Lifetime income replacement is only one reason permanent life insurance is a powerful long-term strategy for financial security.

Permanent life insurance also benefits the insured. A properly constructed and funded life insurance policy gives an insured policyholder a "permission slip" to spend. It allows them to spend down other assets first, knowing funds from their policy will replace assets or generate income as needed. Life insurance gives them financial choices and allows strategic sequencing of asset drawdown in retirement.

The BIG Bonus of Saving:

Typical financial advice speaks of saving an "emergency fund," and yes, emergency funds are essential. (They are so crucial that if you do not have liquid funds to sustain you for a few months, you should save that first.)

But the "goal" of the SureWealthWay is not only to earn 3 or 4% on your savings.

Saving isn't just for emergencies; it's also for opportunities

Saving is just the first step to putting your money to work efficiently. It builds the foundation.

SureWealth strategies increase the velocity of money. The SureWealth Way creates opportunities to accelerate wealth-building with *synergistic strategy*.

Too often, people have their savings and investments tied up in 15 different places where money could be more utilized and accessible. (An IRA or two, a 401(k), a 529 for each child, home equity and others.)

They don't even "see" opportunities because they have no cash to leverage those opportunities.

When people build up their savings and liquidity, new opportunities appear. We can help you discover profitable new strategies you can implement with a lump sum, or you can "build as you go."

The rich get richer because they have prepared. Without ample cash, you won't notice or be able to take advantage of opportunities. You'll also be able to make wiser decisions to stay out of consumer debt. If you don't have cash, financing a brand-new Lexus is easier than purchasing an older one at half-price.

CASE STUDY A:

Nelson Nash, the author of "Becoming Your Own Banker," was in the forestry business before he entered the insurance business. One day, he was able to use his policies to temporarily borrow money for the purchase of land with timber at an excellent, below-market price. The wood was cut and sold, and Nelson made a significant profit from his investment—many times greater than the growth his policy alone was paying.

The opportunity only existed because he had access to capital.

CASE STUDY B:

A client came to a colleague for help with analyzing a commercial real estate deal. It looked like an excellent deal, as the property produced almost 18% cash-on-cash return. However, using his whole life policy for leverage, he could purchase the property with **less** money out of pocket, thereby increasing his effective rate of return to 111%.

His actual cash flow was slightly less than the effective rate, but the rate of return rose because he was now using the life insurance company's money instead of his own. (Greater leverage can increase the rate of return. A "zero-down" deal has an infinite rate of return.) Thus, he also retained the capacity to do more deals and earn more returns at a higher return than if he had only used his cash.

We use calculators to tell "the whole truth" about money, including opportunity costs and other factors often neglected by typical financial advice.

CASE STUDY C:

Cash value policy loans used for private lending contracts provide steady returns of 6.75%-8.5%—guaranteed and fully collateralized. Now, 8% is an excellent rate of return.

Still, when you can borrow against your cash at 6% and earn 8% using the insurance company's capital, that is a 33% improvement or gain. These profits happen while still earning guaranteed gains in your policy and funding other benefits.

Most people think that borrowing at 6% and earning 8% would equal a 2% gain, but that is untrue. You have to think of it in terms of dollars (or widgets may help.) If you buy a widget for $6 and sell it for $8, that is a 33% increase. If you borrow 6 dollars and trade your $6 for someone else's $8, your 6 dollars has earned back an amount equal to 1.33 times itself—a 33-per-cent gain from where you started.

If a store owner buys a hammer for $6 and sells it for $8 retail, they have marked up your product by 33% of its original price. It's no different with dollars. When we can borrow money at one cost and earn it at another, we are simply marking up dollars. Banks make much more money this way – a lot more money. They use other people's money and earn much more on the spread than people realize.

(Not everyone feels comfortable implementing this philosophy, and risks should always be carefully considered. However, this example demonstrates the collateral strategy's power: leveraging savings and other people's money to increase investment returns.)

Remember that when you use whole life insurance as a long-term savings vehicle, you also create a death benefit in place.

Not only do your savings outpace bank rates when held long-term, but in the event of a death, an additional asset is added to your estate that can provide surviving spouses or beneficiaries with tax-free assets or income. (If taken in installments, taxes are paid only on the future interest earned.)

Now you understand why the wealthy still utilize whole life insurance to build and keep wealth. While most investors are told to "buy term and invest the difference," the affluent understand how to use this time-tested product to their advantage.

Example 4: Investing for Growth

Typical financial advice says, "The stock market is the best place to invest long term." However, when you look at the list of Forbes's wealthiest people, you'll discover most of the wealthy built their wealth investing in businesses, not the stock market.

And while you may hear "average" stock market earnings over time are as much as 12%, if we look at the "actual" rates of returns, we discover they are much lower. That's how the math works - average rates of return are misleading.

Let's look at a simple example that emphasizes this point. If an investment doubles one year (100% return) then loses 50% the next, you are back where you started:

$100 x 100% gain = $200
$200 x (50%) = $100

However, if you take an "average" of +100 and negative 50 percent, you come up with 25%.

100 + (50) = 50
50 ÷ 2 years = 25% per year

While this is an extreme example, it demonstrates how "average" rates of return are not the same as actual returns. See "Sequence of Returns" in our book bonus material for a fascinating illustration on this topic. (If you place the returns earned by the S&P 500 in a different sequence, do you get the same result? The answer may shock you!)

https://go.surewealthway.com/bonus

Investor behavior also an enormous difference in Returns. Even when the stock market averages 10 or 12 percent over a period, actual investors might only earn 6 or 7 percent. That is because of the natural tendency to "buy high and sell low."

DALBAR studies investment behavior and compares real-world results with the stock market, such as the S&P 500.

Research shows that investors often chase markets already past their prime or sell stocks during a crash or correction. This leads to lower rates of return that, as you can see in the illustration below, severely impact returns.[23]

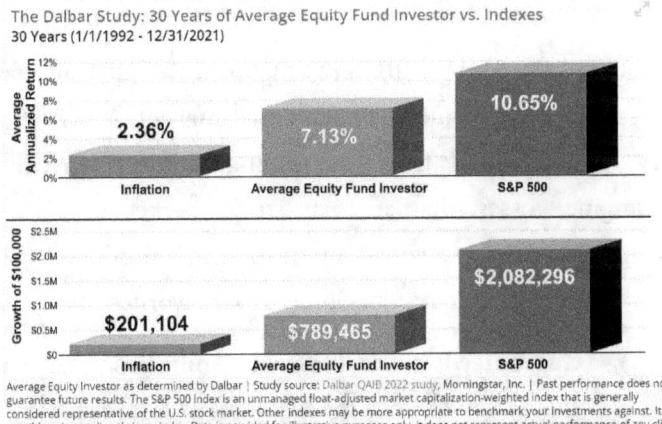

Average Equity Investor as determined by Dalbar | Study source: Dalbar QAIB 2022 study; Morningstar, Inc. | Past performance does not guarantee future results. The S&P 500 Index is an unmanaged float-adjusted market capitalization-weighted index that is generally considered representative of the U.S. stock market. Other indexes may be more appropriate to benchmark your investments against. It is not possible to invest directly in an index. Data is provided for illustrative purposes only. It does not represent actual performance of any client portfolio or account and it should not be interpreted as an indication of such performance. © 2022 Index Fund Advisors, Inc. (IFA.com)

Yet our concerns with the stock market go beyond rates of return, particularly if securities comprise the bulk of an investor's portfolio:

- **Loss of Principal:** Mutual funds and stocks carry high volatility and no guarantees.

---

[23] https://www.ifa.com/articles/dalbar_2016_qaib_investors_still_their_worst_enemy/

- **Loss of Control:** Aside from using stop losses (which are often counter-productive), you have no absolute control over your assets in the stock market.

- **Compounding Fees:** As assets grow, so do fees. Fees are paid whether the investor wins or loses in the stock market.

- **Financial Stress:** What's your peace of mind worth? Market swings can cause stress and anxiety, and following the market can consume your time!

In contrast, SureWealth growth strategies do not have a roller coaster ride with the stock market. You'll never try to build back from devastating, demoralizing, life-changing losses. Rather than stock market drama, we suggest growing your money with products with predictable, reliable results. Some of our favorites include:

- **Guaranteed Fixed-Indexed Annuities** that can expose you to stock market gains without crashes and corrections.

- **Single Premium Whole Life** that—unlike regular whole life—is classified as an investment by the IRS.

- **Real Estate Mortgage Notes** that can create impressive, steady growth in a self-directed IRA.

Let's examine how these strategies provide an alternative to volatile equity markets.

Investing in carefully chosen **Guaranteed Fixed-Indexed Annuities** with tremendous growth potential can expose you to stock market returns without the downside losses. They can also provide steady monthly income with high single-digit, occasionally even low double-digit returns, with virtually no risk.

A Fixed-Indexed Annuity tracks a chosen index, such as the S&P 500. A "participation rate" often indicates whether an annuity reflects all the gains of the index or a portion or percentage of the gains. For instance, a participation rate of 70% would mean that if the index gained 10% one year, the annuity would be credited with 7%, or 70% of the 10% gain.

The contract also sets a "floor" (often 0%) so the annuity never loses value. A floor may also be positive, such as 1% or 2%, or negative, such as (-3%). A ceiling is also set, such as 8, 10, or 12%.

We believe these annuities' real value is what we call "The Gift of Zero," or the ability to eliminate losses. The Gift of Zero is a financial defense for your money, the benefit you gain by your ability to "hold the line" and give up neither principal nor gains.

Warren Buffett calls it Rule #1: "Never lose money!" (Rule #2 is never to forget Rule #1!) Unfortunately, Warren Buffett lost unthinkable sums of money in the Great Recession market crash (through his company, Berkshire Hathaway). He also lost money in the 2020 "quick crash" of the pandemic and he will lose money in the next market crash. Virtually every stock investor loses at times.

As the chart below demonstrates, if you can harness "The Gift of Zero and" never lose your gains, you'll almost always outperform the stock market, at least long-term. Even when you temper the gains, the results are obvious: eliminating risk leads to better results! Even with the sizable gains of the stock market, you are better off protecting your downside and guarding against risk.

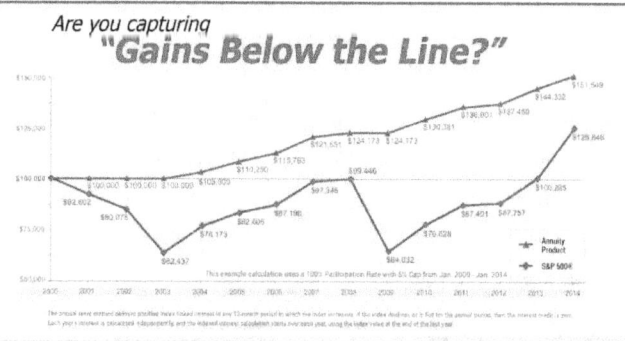

Fixed Indexed Annuity Point-to-Point, Annual Reset Strategy

The chart demonstrates how a **Fixed-Indexed Annuity** might perform compared to the stock market. As you can see, annuities are much more resilient and can deliver more predictable and profitable results.

Life insurance companies provide annuities with long track records of stability.

State insurance commissions regulate the companies that guarantee annuity contracts. Most advisors need to understand annuities better; however, we specialize in them. Book a call today if you'd like to see some of the best annuities and learn how they work in various market conditions. https://go.surewealthway.com/schedule

Single Premium Whole Life is another powerful, often-overlooked strategy. It produces guaranteed growth every year. Even banks use this strategy for high growth.

Banks and other corporations purchase billions of dollars of single-premium life insurance contracts annually from participating (dividend-paying) life insurance companies.

Such corporate or bank policy ownership is known as BOLI (bank-owned life insurance) or COLI (corporate-owned life insurance). Companies deploy this key strategy to ensure payment for employee benefits years down the road. Your household can use this strategy, too. While the corporate bank-owned policies differ slightly from those sold to individuals, they share benefits.

Single Premium Whole Life (SPWL) policies are classified as MECs or Modified Endowment Contracts.

MECs allow the policy owner to use special riders to maximize the amount of cash in the policy beyond the IRS-allowable limit for life insurance. Because of this faster growth, MECs are considered investments.

Yet, like regular Whole Life, MECs also provide a permanent death benefit for beneficiaries. Single Premium Whole Life funded with maximum paid-up addition riders offers a great way to grow cash to those who desire maximum financial security along with living benefits.

- Offered by a highly-rated life insurance company established well over a century ago, Single Premium Whole Life is guaranteed to grow every year. The guaranteed gains and benefits alone compare favorably with any bank product, which is why banks invest in life insurance.
- Cash value dividends of participating mutual insurance companies have historically produced reliable growth and/or income for policyholders. This single Premium Whole Life is an excellent strategy for those who want to grow their nest egg safely to either
- Dividends are not taxed as income, they are use it for themselves or to leave a legacy. considered a return of premium when withdrawn up to basis, and the growth can be borrowed against.

- Single Premium Whole Life includes a rider at no extra charge that allows the insured to advance a portion of the death benefit in case of a terminal, chronic, or specified illness. This provision provides access to additional funds when needed.

- Because mutual insurance companies are owned by the policyholders (as opposed to stock insurance companies owned by stockholders), they plan and invest for the long term rather than just the next quarter. This creates stability and profitability for policyholders.

How can a Single Premium Whole Life policy can grow your nest egg? Reach out to us at 1-877-858-2920 and we'll prepare an analysis for you based on your details (age, health, location, etc.) Most people are blown away when they realize the power of a single premium policy to grow their wealth safely.

Earlier in this chapter, we covered **Real Estate Mortgage Notes**, our favorite strategy for significant cash flow. With a few simple tweaks, mortgage notes can be a powerful asset growth strategy to turbo-charge a retirement account. When placed inside of a self-directed IRA or (preferably) a Roth IRA with interest reinvested, real estate notes produce steady, investment-like returns without subjecting your principal to the unpredictability of the stock market.

What could that unpredictability cost you? Do you really want to take a chance that your finances could fail to provide for your future? Asset growth, reliable income, and financial security depend on your ability to protect yourself from Wall Street risks.

Example #5: Paying for College Education

Typical financial advice tells parents to save in a 529 plan or Coverdell account. Many parents start when their children are born.

Such college savings plans are marketed as the "solution" to save for college, yet these accounts have huge downsides.

- They assist your child in **disqualifying** for financial aid by saving in vehicles that must be declared on a FAFSA application for financial aid. Many students would otherwise qualify for financial assistance.
- They suffer the same problems as other "typical" investments, with high risk, low reward, low control, and limited investment options, often with high or hidden fees.
- They trap dollars in accounts that can only be used for limited reasons with strict rules. (What if they decide not to go to college? In a Coverdell, the child will pay

taxes plus a 10% penalty on earnings if funds are not used within 30 days of their 30th birthday for college expenses.)
- They drain money away from the parents' financial freedom. (Remember opportunity costs? Your child's college education could cost you much more than you think if you save for it the typical way.)
- And now there are even "age-based 529 plans" that share all the same issues and potential instabilities as target-date funds.

Our preferred long-term saving strategy does not have this disadvantage. Nearly all colleges do not count life insurance assets toward the expected family contribution on a financial aid application.

ADDITIONAL OPTIONS FOR COLLEGE:

With a bit of creativity, SureWealth scenarios abound, such as:
- Helping an older child create a business to pay for college.
- Hiring a child in an existing business to help them fund their college education (while producing a tax deduction for the business)
- Purchasing rental property in a college town, a multi-family duplex, triplex, or fourplex that the college-age child can live in and manage. Rental income offsets

living expenses and offers valuable experience while building a real asset.

Whatever options you choose, we recommend choices allowing the student to participate in funding their education in some way, perhaps through work, repayment, or other committments. We have seen this create independence and confidence rather than dependence and entitlement.

We also invite parents to take an honest, open-eyed look at the opportunity costs involved in college. Yes, you may choose to pay for college, even private college or advanced degrees. Still, you should make those choices only after understanding the whole truth about what that will cost you! We can help with this, and we even have special software to help you calculate the actual cost of college education, including opportunity costs. (You don't want to know the answer but need to know.)

As you can see, SureWealth strategies represent a powerful alternative to popular financial advice.

When we stop chasing higher rates of return in a volatile market and focus more on the 10 Truths, we can achieve the financial security we've been pursuing.

SureWealth ideas change the conversation and challenge the questions that typical financial planning and big financial corporations want you to ask:

> *"How much do I need to retire at 65?"*
>
> *"What's the right ratio of stocks to bonds?"*
>
> *"What's the quickest way to pay off a mortgage?"*
>
> *"How much do I need to save to pay for college?"*
>
> *"How can I maximize my qualified plan tax deferrals now?"*

SureWealth strategies turn "conventional wisdom" on its head.

Rather than encouraging you to hand control of your dollars to an advisor, an institution, or the government, SureWealth strategies want you to control your money to use it for your benefit.

Now that you know the Principles and Strategies of the SureWealth Way, what will you do with this information?

CHAPTER 6

What Now?

Once we woke up from our societal-induced dream of typical financial planning built upon Wall-Street strategies, we decided:

To tell everyone who will listen the truth about how money works.

You don't have to give all your dollars to Wall Street. You don't have to cross your fingers and hope the stock market doesn't crash.

It's your money, and you don't have to do everything "they" recommend.

You can choose a different path.

Once you understand the truth about our financial system, there's no going back. We're committed to helping people avoid the rigged system and lousy advice that keeps us from true prosperity.

We can and must learn to build bulletproof, life-long wealth without Wall Street institutions and Big Banks in any economy.

Most people would rather do what everybody else is doing —what they're told to do—than research alternative ways of thinking and doing things. But not you.

If you are reading this, you are an exception, and we'd like to thank you.

Thank you for reading this book, and thank you for taking the time and effort to explore a different way of thinking and doing things.

And now, we have an essential question.

What will you do with this information? Are you using SureWealth principles and strategies (intentionally or not)? How can you align your finances more closely with the 10 Truths of the SureWealth Way? It may be time for you to investigate further. Perhaps it's time to act on what you know to be true. Whatever the case, we encourage you to make changes based on your learning. Decide what your next steps are and make time to take them.

As for me, we're not simply building a business; we're building a movement—the SureWealth Way movement.

We sincerely hope this book's ideas have permanently shifted how you view your finances. Most of all, we hope you can now see the folly of trusting in institutions that work against your best interests.

The financial uncertainty, volatility, and inflation we are heading into may be unprecedented. Many fortunes will be destroyed. Some will lose their retirement funds and have to start from scratch.

What will you do?

Will you take the SureWealth Way?

The stability of our families and the health of our economy require this information to be revealed and utilized.

Can we help you build wealth without the Big Banks, brokerages, and the stock market's roller-coaster ride?

Are you ready to adopt SureWealth thinking and strategies instead of following "typical" financial advice?

Schedule a meeting as soon as possible, and let us help you align your finances for lasting prosperity. Choose a time that works for you. This consultation is free of charge and does not require an obligation.

https://go.surewealthway.com/schedule

We are happy to share additional resources that can help educate about using SureWealth strategies to help build sustainable wealth. But don't wait until you've "learned everything."

Get started with these strategies today before the next market drop. Get your financial forecast and see where your current plan is taking you. Then, discover how to build "Sure Wealth" without Wall Street risks and worries.

Our goal is to improve the certainty of your financial future, adding benefits and guaranteed gains, often with no additional out-of-pocket dollars.

Would you be interested if we could take the same dollars you are currently saving and investing and give you verifiably better results—with guarantees from top-rated insurance companies often included?

If you are already investing in real estate or your own business, would you like to see how you could reduce the cost of capital? Would you like to add financial protections for unexpected setbacks as you do?

We want to show you how you can strategize for any possibility. We want to give you a road map for financial success and stability whether the stock market crashes or soars. We want your family to have strategies that work whether you live, die, or become disabled. It's possible.

We won't promise you overnight riches, unlikely rates of return, or pie-in-the-sky scenarios. But we will give you a step-by-step plan to ensure you'll never be poor.

Ask questions, do your due diligence, and invite your current advisors, lawyer, CFP, or accountant. Everything we do is transparent and verifiable.

There's no high-pressure sales pitch–just information and questions answered. You'll know if we fit because you might realize we have your exact solutions.

We look forward to showing you a better way to wealth.

Meet the Author

Andy Daniels
Founder
Andy@surewealthllc.com

"I am Inspired by the opportunity to help you grow your wealth without the unnecessary risk and volatility of stocks, real estate, and other traditional investments. With SureWealth, you take control of your finances to reach your financial goals and dreams. What we do has been called a 'secret weapon' by our clients. Let us be that for you.

Welcome to the SureWealth Way Workbook

This specially offered workbook is our way of thanking you for purchasing a copy of The Sure Wealth Way. It was designed to help you intentionally and purposefully implement the guiding principles and strategies of the SureWealth Way philosophy in your own financial planning.

By following the steps and exercises provided, you will better understand your financial situation, set meaningful goals, and develop actionable strategies to achieve financial security and independence.

Overview of Sections

This workbook is divided into four main sections, each focusing on a crucial aspect of financial planning and management according to the SureWealth Way principles.

1. **Organizing Financial Information (Pages 2-7):**

   - This section helps you gather and organize all relevant financial information, including your accounts, income, expenses, debts, and insurance policies. Accurate and thorough documentation of your financial data is the foundation of effective financial planning.

2. **Identifying and Refining Financial Goals (Pages 8-11):**

   - Setting clear, achievable financial goals is essential for success. In this section, you will learn how to define SMART goals and create a structured system to review and refine these goals regularly. You will develop a roadmap for your financial future by breaking down your objectives into actionable steps.

3. **Current and Future Lifestyle Planning (Pages 12-14):**
   - Planning for your current and future lifestyle involves creating a monthly expense plan and preparing for significant life events and large expenditures. This section provides templates and strategies to help you manage your finances effectively through different stages of life.

4. **Financial Strategies Implementation (Pages 15-18):**
   - The final section focuses on applying SureWealth strategies to your financial planning. You will learn how to use whole life policies for safe-money storage, project retirement savings, manage debt payments, and optimize tax strategies. These tools will help you create a secure and predictable financial future.

By working through each section of this workbook, you will build a comprehensive and personalized financial plan aligned with the SureWealth Way philosophy. Let's get started on the path to greater financial security and peace of mind!

Organizing Financial Information

Personal Information
Use the tables below to fill in your personal and family details. Accurate information here will help you keep track of essential data needed for your financial planning.

Personal Details

Name	
Date of Birth/Age	
Occupation	
Social Security Number	
Address	
Daytime Phone	
Evening Phone	
Email	
Marital Status	

Spouse/Partner Information

Name	
Date of Birth/Age	
Occupation	
Social Security Number	
Daytime Phone	
Evening Phone	
Email	

Children/Grandchildren Information

Name	Date of Birth/Age	Years to College	Estimated Tuition/Yr

Additional Notes:

Potential Retirement Assets

Use this table to list all your potential retirement assets, their associated companies, and the amounts. This will help you gather all your financial information in one place.

Asset Type	Owner	Company Name	Amount
401(k) Plans			
IRA Accounts			
Roth IRA Accounts			
Savings Accounts			
Brokerage Accounts			
Life Insurance Policies (Cash Value)			
Annuities			
Social Security Benefits			
Pension Plans			
Real Estate Investments			
Other Assets			

Additional Notes:

Income and Expenses

Use the tables below to document your income sources and monthly expenses accurately. This section will help you understand your cash flow and identify areas where you can optimize your spending and saving.

Annual Income

List all sources of annual income for you and your spouse/partner. Include details about any fluctuations, bonuses, or other relevant information.

Income Source	Me	Spouse/Partner	Total
Salary/Wages			
Bonuses			
Business Income			
Investment Income			
Social Security			
Pension			
Rental Income			
Other:			

Income Details

Detail	Me	Spouse/Partner	Total
Current Year Gross Wages			
Taxes Owed /Refund			
Bonuses Expected)			
Interest & Dividends			

Monthly Expenses

List your monthly expenses in detail to get a clear picture of your spending. This will help you manage your budget and identify areas for potential savings.

Expense Category	Amount
Housing (Rent/Mortgage)	
Utilities	
Groceries/Food	
Transportation (Gas, Insurance)	
Insurance (Health, Life, etc.)	
Debt Payments (Credit Cards, Loans)	
Entertainment	
Savings Contributions	
Investments	
Childcare/Education	
Medical Expenses	
Miscellaneous	

Additional Notes:

Debt Information

Document all your debts, including mortgages, loans, and credit card balances. Include details about interest rates, balances, and monthly payments.

Debt Type	Balance	Monthly Payment	Interest Rate
Mortgage			
Home Equity Loan			
Credit Card 1			
Credit Card 2			
Car Loan			
Student Loan			
Other Loan			

Additional Notes:

Retirement Accounts

In this section, list all details regarding your retirement accounts. This will help you track your savings and make informed decisions about your retirement planning.

Retirement Account Details

Account Type	My Total	Spouse Total	Contribution	Employer Match	Rate of Return
401(k)					
Traditional IRA					
Roth IRA					
SEP IRA					
SIMPLE IRA					
Other					

Additional Notes:

Contribution History and Future Plans

Detail	Me	Spouse/Partner	Amount
Percentage of Income Contributed			
Have you adjusted your contribution amount? (Yes/No)			
If yes, why?			
Planned Future Contribution Changes			
Tax Obligation on Early Withdrawal			
Expected Rate of Return over the Next 25 Years			
Historical Rate of Return Since Start			

Retirement Planning

Detail	Me	Spouse/Partner
Desired Retirement Age		
Desired Annual Income in Retirement		
Expected Sources of Retirement Income		
How diversified is your retirement plan? (Scale 1-10)		
Retirement Lifestyle Plans (e.g., part-time work, travel)		

Social Security and Pension Estimates

This section will help you document your Social Security and pension estimates. Understanding these sources of income is crucial for comprehensive retirement planning.

Social Security Estimates

Detail	Me	Spouse/Partner
Estimated Monthly Benefit at Full Retirement Age		
Estimated Monthly Benefit at Early Retirement (Age 62)		
Estimated Monthly Benefit at Delayed Retirement (Age 70)		
Date of Last Estimate		

Note: To obtain an estimate of your Social Security benefits, visit SSA.gov and set up an account.

Pension Plan Details

Pension Plan	Me	Spouse/Partner	Estimated Monthly Benefit	Vesting Status
Pension Plan 1				
Pension Plan 2				
Other Pension				

Pension Estimates and Vesting

Detail	Me	Spouse/Partner
Years of Service Required for Full Vesting		
Years of Service Completed		
Earliest Age to Start Receiving Benefits		
Expected Monthly Benefit at Earliest Retirement Age		
Expected Monthly Benefit at Full Retirement Age		

Additional Notes:

Insurance Policies

This section will help you document your insurance policies, including life, health, and other types of insurance. Keeping track of these details ensures that you and your family are adequately covered.

Life Insurance Policies

Policy Type	Policy Holder	Company Name	Policy Number
Whole Life Insurance			
Term Life Insurance			
Universal Life Insurance			
Other			

Policy Number	Coverage Amount	Cash Value	Premium Amount/Frequency

Health Insurance Policies

Policy Type	Company Name	Policy Number	Premium Amount
Health Insurance			
Dental Insurance			
Vision Insurance			
Other			

Disability Insurance

Policy Type	Company Name	Policy Number	Coverage Amount	Premium Amount
Short-Term Disability				
Long-Term Disability				

Additional Notes:

Long-Term Care Insurance

Policy Type	*Company Name*	*Policy Number*	*Coverage Amount*	*Premium Amount*
Long-Term Care				

Other Insurance Policies

Policy Type	*Company Name*	*Policy Number*	*Premium Amount*
Auto Insurance			
Homeowners Insurance			
Renters Insurance			
Umbrella Insurance			
Other			

Additional Notes:

Investments and Other Assets

This section helps you document all your investments and other assets. Accurate documentation will aid in understanding your overall financial position and planning effectively for the future.

Investment Accounts

Account Type	Account Holder	Company Name	Account Number	Current Value
Brokerage				
Mutual Funds				
Stocks				
Bonds				
ETFs				
Other				

Real Estate Investments

Property Type	Location	Current Value	Mortgage Balance	Income
Primary Residence				
Rental Property 1				
Rental Property 2				
Vacation Home				
Commercial Property				
Other				

Other Assets

Asset Type	Owner	Current Value
Savings Bonds		
Certificates of Deposit (CDs)		
Precious Metals		
Collectibles		
Vehicles		
Business Interests		
Other		

Additional Notes:

Tax Returns and Financial Documents

This section will help you gather and organize your recent tax returns and other important financial documents. Keeping these documents accessible and organized is crucial for effective financial planning and making informed decisions.

Tax Returns

Tax Year	Filed By (Self/Spouse/Joint)	Total Income	Adjusted Gross Income (AGI)	Total Tax Paid	Refund/Amount Owed
2021					
2020					
2019					
2018					

Additional Notes:

Important Financial Documents

Enter a checkmark once these documents are stored in an easily accessible location

Document	Me	Spouse/Partner
Pay Stubs or Current Income Estimates		
Mortgage Statements		
Property Value Estimates		
Credit Card Statements		
Loan Statements		
Bank Account Statements (Checking/Savings)		
Investment Account Statements		
Retirement Account Statements		
Life Insurance Policies		
Annuity Contracts		
Record of Untaxed Income (e.g., Social Security)		
Business or Farm Income Tax Returns		
Other:		

Identifying and Refining Financial Goals

Introduction to Goal Setting

To achieve long-term success, it is essential to set clear and achievable financial goals. We've defined your financial goals using the SMART criteria (Specific, Measurable, Achievable, Relevant, Time-bound). Break down your objectives into actionable steps to create a structured plan that can achieve your financial dreams.

Defining Your Financial Goals

Short-Term Goals (1-5 Years)

Goal	Specific Details	Amount Needed	Target Date
Example: Build Emergency Fund	Save $1,000 per month until $12,000 is saved	$12,000	12 months

Medium-Term Goals (5-10 Years)

Goal	*Specific Details*	*Amount Needed*	*Target Date*
Example: Pay Off Car Loan	Make extra payments to pay off loan in 5 years	$15,000	5 years

Long-Term Goals (10+ Years)

Goal	*Specific Details*	*Amount Needed*	*Target Date*
Example: Retirement Fund	Contribute $500 per month to retirement account	$200,000	20 years

Progressive Goal Refinement

As you define your goals, use the following templates to break them down into actionable steps. This will help you create a detailed plan and track your progress.

Goal Breakdown Template

Goal	Step	Action Required	Target Date
Example: Build Emergency Fund	Step 1: Open Savings Account	Open a high-interest savings account at local bank	1 week
	Step 2: Set Up Direct Deposit	Arrange for automatic transfer of $1,000 monthly	1 month
	Step 3: Review Progress	Check account balance and adjust if necessary	Monthly

Regular Goal Review System

Set up a system to regularly review and adjust your goals. This ensures you stay on track and make necessary adjustments based on your progress and any changes in your circumstances.

Review Frequency	Date
Monthly	
Quarterly	
Annually	

Additional Notes:

Current and Future Lifestyle Planning

Introduction to Lifestyle Planning

Planning for your current and future lifestyle is a crucial part of financial planning. This section will help you create a monthly expense plan and prepare for significant life events and large expenditures, ensuring you have a comprehensive understanding of your financial needs and goals.

Monthly Expense Plan

Use this template to document and manage your monthly expenses; you may identify where you can save!

Monthly Expenses

Expense Category	Amount
Housing (Rent/Mortgage)	
Utilities (Electric, Water, Gas)	
Groceries/Food	
Transportation (Gas, Insurance)	
Insurance (Health, Life, Auto)	
Debt Payments (Credit Cards, Loans)	
Entertainment	
Savings Contributions	
Investments	
Childcare/Education	
Medical Expenses	
Miscellaneous	
Total Monthly Expenses	

Large Planned Expenses

Plan for significant life events and large expenditures by documenting your expected costs and savings strategies.

Planned Large Expenses

Expense	Estimated Cost	Target Date	Savings Strategy
Purchase a Home			
Children's College Education			
Major Vacation			
Home Renovations			
Downsize at Retirement			
Other			

Additional Notes:

Future Lifestyle Changes

Prepare for future lifestyle changes by planning your expenses and understanding how they will impact your budget.

Future Lifestyle Plans

Lifestyle Change	Estimated Cost	Target Date	Plan to Cover Costs
Retirement			
Part-Time Work			
Travel			
New Hobbies			
Relocation			
Other			

Additional Notes:

Introduction to Financial Strategies

This section will guide you through applying SureWealth strategies to your financial planning. You will learn how to use whole life policies for safe-money storage, project retirement savings, manage debt payments, and optimize tax strategies. These tools will help you create a secure and predictable financial future.

Whole Life Policy as Safe-Money Storage

Understand how properly structured whole-life policies can be used for safe-money storage, providing benefits like guaranteed growth, tax advantages, and protection from creditors.

Whole Life Policy Calculation

Detail	Me	Spouse/Partner
Current Policy Value		
Annual Premium		
Death Benefit		
Cash Value Growth Rate		
Loan Availability		

Sequence of Returns

Plan for the impact of market conditions on your retirement savings by projecting different scenarios based on your retirement age and withdrawal rates.

Retirement Savings Projection

Detail	Age	Initial Balance	Annual Withdrawal	Expected Rate of Return	Projected Balance
Early Retirement (Age 62)					
Full Retirement Age (67)					
Delayed Retirement (Age 70)					

Debt Service Transfer

Compare the benefits of transferring your annual debt service from external banks to your own self-funded store of capital. This includes paying off loans and then making payments back to yourself.

Debt Service Comparison

Debt Type	Current Annual Payment	Self-Funded Annual Payment	Savings
Mortgage			
Credit Card			
Car Loan			
Student Loan			
Other			

Tax Strategies

Evaluate the impact of different tax strategies, including paying taxes upfront versus deferring them, on your overall wealth.

Tax Strategy Comparison

Strategy	Tax Rate	Impact on Wealth
Pay Taxes Upfront		
Defer Taxes to Later		

Putting It All Together

Congratulations on completing the SureWealth Way Workbook! By organizing your financial information, setting and refining your goals, planning for your current and future lifestyle, and implementing SureWealth strategies, you have taken significant steps towards achieving financial security and independence.

Next Steps

Review Your Workbook:

Ensure all sections are complete and reflect your current financial situation and goals.

Make any necessary adjustments based on your regular goal review system.

Implement Your Plan:

Start taking actionable steps based on the strategies outlined in this workbook.

Monitor your progress and adjust your plan as needed.

Seek Professional Guidance:

Financial planning can be complex, and having a professional to guide you can be invaluable.

Consider reaching out to a SureWealth Strategist for personalized assistance and advice.

Reach out to a SureWealth Strategist for help implementing your plan and to ensure you are on the right path toward financial security. We will provide expert guidance and support tailored to your unique financial situation and goals.

Scan the QR Code Below to Connect with a SureWealth Strategist:

https://about.thesurewealthway.com/schedule

Thank you for choosing the SureWealth Way. We wish you success on your journey to financial freedom and security.

We Value Your Feedback!

Share Your Experience

Thank you for taking the time to complete the SureWealth Way Workbook. We value your journey toward financial security and independence and hope this workbook has provided valuable insights and actionable steps to help you achieve your goals.

We would love to hear about your experience using the SureWealth Way Workbook. Your feedback is essential in helping us improve our materials and support others on their financial journeys.

Leave a Review

Please take a moment to share your thoughts and experiences. Your review can help others understand the benefits of the SureWealth Way and how it can improve their financial planning.

https://about.thesurewealthway.com/review

We Value Your Feedback!

Scan the QR Code Below to Leave Your Review:

What to Include in Your Review

- How the book helped you organize your financial information.
- Your experience with setting and refining your financial goals.
- The impact of the SureWealth strategies on your financial planning.
- Any specific features or sections that you found particularly useful.
- Suggestions for improvement or additional topics you would like to see.

Thank You!

Your feedback is invaluable to us, and we appreciate your time and effort in sharing your thoughts. Together, we can continue to enhance the SureWealth Way and support more individuals in achieving financial security and independence.

https://go.surewealthway.com/review

www.ingramcontent.com/pod-product-compliance
Lightning Source LLC
Chambersburg PA
CBHW071053240526
45471CB00015B/1832